Yet I Will Praise Him

Our Spiritual Odyssey of Living with Crohn's Disease

Bev and Dorsey Burk with Krystin Burk Carlson

EXPANDED EDITION

Copyright 2019 by Dorsey Burk

ISBN 9781090983442

All Scripture quotations in this book are from the King James Version of the Holy Bible unless otherwise identified.

All rights reserved. No portion of this publication by reproduced, stored in an electronic system, or transmitted in any form or by any means, electronic, mechanical, photocopy, recording, or otherwise, without the prior permission of the author. Brief quotations may be used in literary reviews.

Dedication

To the third and fourth generation:

Abigayle LeAnn
Rebekkah Michelle
Alexis Alice
Crysellyn René
Javan Paul
Samara Christine
Kaidyn Jhené

Author's Note

Bev's journey ended at 12:37 on the afternoon of October 30, 2018. I had already written several chapters of this expanded version of *Yet I Will Praise Him* and was waiting for Bev to write the alternating chapters. However, June through October was filled with appointments, travel, special meetings, and General Conference. She never had time to write. Consequently, I asked my daughter Krystin to help fill in the gaps, based on conversations with her mother.

Table of Contents

Introduction	7
1. Dorsey: First Steps	11
2. Bev: The Beginning	19
3. Dorsey: Missionaries in Germany	29
4. Bev: Living in Germany	33
5. Dorsey: Living Our Dream	41
6. Bev: From Germany to St. Louis	51
7. Dorsey: The Road Gets Rougher	59
8. Bev: The Promise	73
9. Dorsey: More Challenges and Adjustments	89
10. Bev and Dorsey: Lessons from the Journey	99
11. Dorsey: The Journey Continues	107
12. For Bev: International Traveler	113
13. Dorsey: Life, Death, and Social Security	119
14. For Bev: Miracles	123
15. Dorsey: More Fields	127
16. For Bev: Retreats	131
17. Dorsey: Heart Surgery #2	135
18. For Bev: Heart Surgery Again	139
19. Dorsey: 2016–2017	145
20. Krystin's View	149

21. Dorsey: 2018	151
22. For Bev: Gattex	155
23. Dorsey: Victory	159
24. Krystin's View	167
25. Krystin: A Lesson and a Promise	171
26. Dorsey: An Afterword	175

Introduction

"She's awesome!" "She inspires me!" and "She's a walking miracle" are probably the three most common expressions I hear when someone is talking about my wife. I smile, voice my agreement, and give glory to God for the forty-seven plus years I have lived with Beverly Jeannene Sponsler Burk. She's an amazing woman whose life testifies to God's faithfulness.

Perhaps a former leader of the Daughters of Zion prayer ministry at New Life St. Louis summed it up best in a thank-you note to my wife:

*Sister Burk, I read recently that a sign of a good leader is to enlist people smarter than you. If that's what makes a good leader, I qualify! I'm so thankful that someone smarter that I am (you!) has agreed to help me! Thanks for working with me as a team. You are **awesome**, and I appreciate **you** very much. Thanks for being so wonderful! And I sincerely mean that! Carolyn Little*

I totally agree with Carolyn Little and my wife's many fans. She is one fantastic lady! (See Proverbs 31:28).

As one who has been with her in the good times and the bad, I know her better than most. That is why I am helping her write this book. In doing so, we hope to share two difference perspectives and spiritual insights that we have gleaned on our odyssey with Crohn's disease. We may repeat details and do a little backtracking as we write alternating chapters. However, some of this is intentional so we can give the viewpoint of both the sick person and the caregiver.

For those not acquainted with the Crohn's disease, it is a member of the family of inflammatory bowel diseases (IBS) and can affect any part of the gastrointestinal tract from the mouth to the anus. However, it primarily attacks the lower part of the small intestine, the ileum. In about a third of the cases, the colon is also affected.

Crohn's disease may be considered a cousin to ulcerative colitis. Whereas ulcerative colitis causes ulceration and inflammation in the colon and rectum, the inflammation caused by Crohn's extends into the deeper layers of the intestinal wall. The inflammation tends to thicken the bowel wall with swelling and fibrous scar tissue, thus narrowing the passage. The disease may also cause deep ulcer tracts that burrow all the way through the bowel wall into surrounding tissue, into adjacent segments of intestine, into other nearby organs, or into the skin.

Although the frequency of this chronic disease seems to be increasing, the disease is relatively rare. The Mayo Clinic estimates that only one to five people out of ten thousand have Crohn's disease. (See www.mayohealth.-org/mayo/askphys/qa960707.htm 2000.) The cause of the disease is unknown, and therefore no medical cure exists. The goals of medical treatment are to suppress the inflammation, permit healing of the tissue, and relieve the symptoms of fever, diarrhea, and abdominal pain. (See www.ccfa.or/Physical/crohnsb.html 2000.)

As Bev once wrote, "My experience with Crohn's disease was hard and trying, sometimes frustrating and discouraging, yet at the same time encouraging, rewarding, and satisfying." Please join us on our turbulent trek. We both know it has been well worth the trip.

Chapter 1

Dorsey: First Steps

Before we get too far into the journey, some background information is in order.

Bev and I first met in May 1967. Having won that year's Sheaves for Christ scholarship to Conquerors Bible College (CBC) in Portland, Oregon, I was visiting the school over Memorial Day weekend. The college choir was singing that Sunday night at Neighborhood United Pentecostal Church, a home missions work pastored by George Sponsler, Bev's dad. I went to hear the choir.

In the process I met Bev. She was wearing a burgundy and gray plaid suit with box pleats in the skirt—because her mother thought they made her look thinner—and horribly ugly horn-rimmed glasses. I wish her impression of me had been as favorable. It wasn't. In fact, when the new school year started, and I began dating one of her best friends, she said, "Surely, Priscilla, you can do better than *that!*

The following year Bev came to CBC, and we both worked with Priscilla at the library processing unit for Portland Public Schools. For the next two years we attended classes together, ate together, rode to work together, and went to church together on Wednesday nights. She became my best friend. I could talk to her about anything, including girl problems. She always had a listening ear.

During my senior year, the opportunity arose for me to complete my ministerial internship—the college's hands-on, fourth-year program—in Germany under missionary Wayne Nigh. Brother Nigh had been the dean of men at CBC. He had also baptized Bev when she was nine years old, and he was the Oregon District youth president. His wife, Esther, had been the college's cook—baking fresh cinnamon rolls for the morning break and dinner rolls for the noon meal—and, as the dean of women, had a positive influence on Bev.

One night toward the end of the school year, Bev and I called the Nighs in Germany. Suddenly, I realized she cared about the same things as I did. Somehow the prospects of leaving my best friend for a nine-month internship lost some of its glamour and appeal. In the ensuing hours, I realized that I had found more than a friend. I had found someone to love and with whom to share my life's ambitions. My newfound revelation was a shocking but delightful development!

My proposal at Multnomah Falls took Bev completely by surprise. Instead of saying, "Yes! Oh yes!" she simply said, "You haven't told me that you love me." She was right. I just somehow expected her to know how I felt even though we had rarely actually dated until that night. (After all, we were in Bible school, and, in signing the date request forms, we had agreed to "cheerfully" abide by all the school's rules!) I finally convinced her of my love, and she agreed to accompany me wherever the will of God took us.

We announced our engagement following CBC's 1970 commencement service. Priscilla grinned as she walked toward us and said, "Surely, Bev, you can do better than *that*!"

Rev. and Mrs. George Sponsler, parents of the bride, Bride and Groom, Mrs. Arbie Burk, mother of the groom

Following my internship in Germany under Wayne Nigh, C. H. Yadon and Bev's dad, George Sponsler, joined us in holy matrimony on June 26, 1971. We began our married life assisting Pastor Joe Dinwiddie at the twenty-five-member First Pentecostal Church in Klamath

Falls, Oregon. When the hours of my part-time job were cut, we moved back to Portland. I worked at the Coats and Clark thread warehouse across the street from CBC and did some promotional work for the college. Bev and I both became active in her dad's church. In mid-1973 Paul Box, the secretary of Foreign Missions, called to ask if we would be interested in teaching in the Bible school in Jamaica.

We had felt a missionary call to Germany for a few years. Nevertheless, we walked through the door that God had opened and celebrated our daughter's first birthday the day after we arrived in the beautiful island. Looking back, we realize that God was preparing us for future ministry. The six months in Jamaica proved to us that we could adapt to cultural changes and be happy in the will of God, regardless of where it would lead.

We loved Jamaica and learned many valuable lessons while working under the leadership of Paul and Beth Reynolds, the resident United Pentecostal Church missionaries. The intensity of worship at Pentecostal Tabernacle on Wildman Street, the humility and sincerity of the members, their willingness to sacrifice for a new building, and Bishop Reynolds's ministry of the Word made any hardship we might have endured a small price to pay for the blessings we received. We went to teach in the Bible school, but the Jamaicans taught us much more than we taught our students. We were the ones who really profited.

Following Christmas 1974, we moved to St. Louis. On January 2, 1975, I became the finance secretary for the Foreign Missions Division. Working under the direction of Paul Box, I processed all requisitions from the missionaries, made sure they received their monthly allotment, and handled the financial records of the division. While I enjoyed my job, we could not get away from the call to Germany. We made application to meet the Foreign Missions Board in October 1976.

The 1976 General Conference was in Anaheim, California. Bev flew out to Portland a few weeks before conference, taking our four-year-old daughter and our five-month-old son to visit their grandparents. During that time, she began bleeding rectally. We both thought it was from the stress of our applying for appointment.

Another couple with more ministerial experience than we had was appointed to Germany at the conference. Extremely disappointed, we licked our wounds and considered our options. While one offer was attractive and very tempting, we felt it was the will of God for us to continue in the Foreign Missions Division.

As the weeks passed, Bev's bleeding continued. Dr. David Berwald, a fine young surgeon who was taking over his father's practice, finally diagnosed the problem as granulomatous colitis, commonly called Crohn's disease, an intestinal disease akin to ulcerative colitis. Although he was not well acquainted with the disease at the time, he attended special seminars to learn as much as he could. Bev was his thirty-second patient in his new office.

He assured us that the disease was treatable with medication and that, unlike ulcerative colitis, it was not known to become cancerous. He also asserted that going to Germany should not adversely affect the disease since

Germany has modern medicine. In our ignorance, we rejoiced and applied to meet the Foreign Missions Board at the 1977 General Conference in Indianapolis.

That October, we were one of thirteen couples appointed as United Pentecostal Church missionaries. We were elated! Our dreams were coming true. It felt so good to be in the will of God.

The following weeks blurred as we transitioned from Foreign Missions Division employee to fully appointed missionary on deputation. We reduced our earthly possessions to six fifty-gallon drums that we packed for storage and later shipping to Germany. I cleared out my office at World Evangelism Center, and we drove to Portland for the Christmas holidays. Our deputation services would begin the first week of 1978.

Traveling with an active eighteen-month toddler and a five-year-old is a real trip! When we were hoping that our darlings would woo a Partner in Missions commitment from the local pastor, Krystin would turn shy and refuse to speak to him or Devon would throw up on the wife's new drapes. Some pastors' wives thought we were too harsh with the children; others thought we were too lenient. We thanked God time and time again for the twenty-seven-foot motorhome we called home. It gave us some privacy and allowed the children to have their own beds.

Many times during our eleven months of travel, Bev was ill but valiantly tried to cover her distress. Often the food she ate would not stay down. Frequently she would double over in extreme pain. Again we laid the blame on the stress caused by travel and assured ourselves that things would be better when we settled in Germany.

Chapter 2
Bev: The Beginning

I once read a book about Pentecostal courtship and had to scratch my head. Not one of the contributors admitted to thinking their God-intended, lifelong companion reminded them of a banty rooster! Almost all the writers had been drawn to the "man of God." It just wasn't that way for us. However, as the first impressions faded and a friendship grew, I realized Dorsey Burk was a very nice guy. I was certainly surprised.

At the end of two years, it dawned on me as he was preparing to leave for Germany that half of me would be going. No stars zinged their way across the sky. No bells chimed, no fireworks lit up in my head—I just had an overwhelming sense of incompleteness.

No romance writer would have used a relationship like ours in a book. It had been a progression from turned-up noses to friendship to love. The romance came later, and I'm glad it did. If our love had been based only on physical attraction, I'm not sure that could have sustained us during the storms that followed.

Thankfully, time takes care of some matters. We became engaged. Dorsey went to Germany. I finished my senior year at Conquerors Bible College. He came home. We got married and moved to Klamath Falls, Oregon.

When Dorsey's hours at his job were cut back, the only door open was to move back to Portland, work in my dad's church in whatever capacity became available, and have a baby. And then we ended up . . . in Jamaica!

I don't think Jamaica was nearly as pivotal for Dorsey as it was for me. Missionary Beth Reynolds had that philosophy of "Well, my dear, of course you can do it!" Jamaica was a time of foundational solidification for me as a young minister's wife. Many times, in later years, I would face an experience I wasn't looking forward to and think, *Is there a job to do? If so, then you can do it. You just have to figure out how. And if the figuring doesn't work, take the one step in front of you and continue until the job is done!*

Moving to St. Louis in late December 1974 began one of the darkest periods of my life. Being the pastor's daughter of a home missions work, I was used to being in the middle of everything. If I wasn't bossing a project, I was helping to boss it—a vocation that I was extremely good at! Now we were in a big church. I did not feel accepted, and no one cared about my opinions on anything. It was a very bitter pill to swallow, and I sank into deep depression.

Two things happened that changed my attitude. First, I received a bouquet of flowers. I called everyone I could think of—everyone whom I thought would do such an act of kindness. No one ever took the credit for those flowers, but suddenly I realized that someone, somewhere cared.

The second event was something I did for myself. After the flowers came, I realized how very depressed I had been and decided to take control of the situation. First, I prayed for power over such debilitating depression. Second, I took a broom and swept our entire apartment. I swept the ceiling, the walls, and the furniture—everything in Jesus' name. I swept it all into a little pile in front of the door, opened the doorway, and swept it out in Jesus' name.

Instantly, the depression left. From that point on, I felt accepted everywhere. And although at times it still seemed that on one wanted my opinions, I felt loved. I found avenues to work in; I sought areas in which I could minister.

Devon Paul joined Krystin as a part of our family on May 2, 1976. His twinkling eyes, his white-blond hair, and his ready smile completed our family. All our married life we had planned to go to Germany, and we were ready.

During our deputation travel, I started having severe abdominal pains—often severe enough to cause me to double over. This usually occurred two or three hours after eating and only seemed to be relieved by vomiting, thereby lessening the tightness in my stomach. I thought the extreme pressure a traveling missionary is under was taking its toll on my body and that things would certainly be fine when we got settled in Europe.

The day finally came to say goodbye to our family and friends in America and hello to our new homeland. It was love at first sight! Germany was much more wonderful than I ever thought possible. We soon found an apartment, bought furniture, started language school, and settled six-year-old Krystin in school. Life was wonderful—except for my health.

Leaving for Germany from Portland International Airport (PDX), December 28, 1978

Many days I could not keep anything on my stomach. I had such severe cramps that I would awaken my husband by groaning in my sleep. I would lie in bed day after day on a heating pad, trying somehow to stop the pain. I took strong pain pills, but nothing seemed to give any relief. When I was able to get up to do a few things, often I would have to hold to the wall or furniture. My weight plummeted to ninety-seven pounds

Photo from Bev's German driver's license

My German doctor finally put me in the Women's Clinic of the University Hospital in Wiesbaden for very painful tests, which were repeated over and over. A psychologist came to find out why I would ask the doctors what they were going to do that day and why.

Finally, the wonderful day came when I went home. I was no better, nor had they told me anything about my disease. I was simply sent home without one word. However, I was more than happy to leave any way that I could.

Up to this point I have not mentioned God. There is a basic reason for this rather obvious omission. I had not allowed Him to be involved. I was handling this. If the German doctors were correct, if all of this was caused by tension, if I was too intense about life, then all could be cured by relaxing. I really tried to do all that I was told. But I kept going, without asking God for His direct help. I was strong willed, and I felt I could do whatever was necessary if I really made up my mind to do it.

Soon after I came home from the hospital, a strange thing happened. For three nights in a row, I dreamed I was in an airplane, my spirit was very heavy, and somehow I realized I was taking an emergency leave. Next to me sat a woman in a brown, flowered silk dress. I did not understand this at all.

In May 1979, my mother called from her hospital room in Portland, Oregon. She had just been told that she had cancer and had only six to nine months to live. We had no idea she was even ill. For days, I went around in shock. Should I go home? Should I wait? What could be done? All during this time I was still extremely weak.

Sometimes there is one incident in life that changes an entire story. Mine came one day when I had cried until I was too weak to cry any more. I was sitting in the living room—not thinking, not crying, just sitting. I had put some records on the stereo, trying to collect myself. One of Bill Gaither's songs suddenly caught my attention. The words were:

> I will praise Him,
> Knowing that my praise
> Will cost me everything.
> I will praise Him,
> Praise Him with the joy
> That comes from knowing
> That I have held back nothing.
> And He is Lord.
> He is Lord.
> HE IS LORD!

Praise! To praise, not holding back anything at all? Praise, knowing it would cost everything I had? This sounded impossible, but sitting in Wiesbaden, Germany, on that day in May, I knew that somehow I had to learn how.

I sat crying and praying. That day I told God I had no idea how to accomplish this task, but if He would guide me, I would do all I could to learn. I began thanking Him that I had such terrible nerve problems; I was a wreck and had made myself that way. Next, I thanked Him for my mother's illness; that I had a sixteen-year-old sister whom He would have to care for and help grow up; and that my father was going to have to try to pastor a church, teach full time in public school, raise Lurissa, and still try to stay sane. Needless to say, I did not sound very thankful, but it was a start. I felt a burden lift, and I knew that was the answer I had been looking for.

The next day, I was once again unable to leave my bed, but it was with a different attitude. I thanked God—really thanked Him—and life was good. During that day, I thumbed through the Book of Psalms. I was impressed by the many times David said, "I will." "I will praise the LORD" (Psalm 7:17). "I will praise thee" (Psalm 9:1). "I will be glad . . . I will sing praise" (Psalm 9:2). Throughout the psalms, the theme was the same: I have problems, but I will praise.

Starting to learn by praising for everything seemed a little too difficult. So I started by going one hour, stopping, kneeling, or if I was confined to bed that day, bowing my head and praising God for everything that had happened during the previous hour. Soon I could praise God for all that had happened during that time span. I could praise Him that I had to hold the wall and try to dust. I could praise Him that I could eat two or three bites of supper. I could praise Him that those two or three bites of supper had not stayed down.

Praise changed everything. I became happy, almost excited. Even when I was very sick, I still could learn to look for things to praise God for. It became an all-consuming task.

One day I was extremely week. Several people had told me how terrible I looked and how I really needed to gain weight. I knew that. But I also knew that I could not keep anything down long enough to get any nutritional value from it. I started reading the Bible to receive some encouragement from somewhere.

I opened to Psalm 41: "Blessed is he that considereth the poor: the Lord will deliver him in time of trouble. The Lord will preserve him, and keep him alive; and he shall be blessed upon the earth: and thou wilt not deliver him unto the will of his enemies. The Lord will strengthen him upon the bed of languishing. . . . An evil disease, say they, cleaveth fast unto him: and now that he lieth he shall rise up no more."

I could not believe what I was reading! It sounded as if David had been with me the last few days! That chapter became the fort to which I would run whenever I felt discouraged, and I would find comfort there.

Roman 8:28 also changed me. I had read and memorized this verse as a child. I had read and memorized it as a teenager. I had read and memorized it as a young adult. But when I started to praise God for it, I learned how to use it. I thanked God that whatever this disease was and whatever it involved, it was for my good. I really started to appreciate the lessons I was learning from it.

Chapter 3

Dorsey: Missionaries in Germany

We cleared German immigration on December 29, 1978, and immediately went to Schloss Freudenberg, the old palace in Wiesbaden that served as the headquarters church and Bible school facility.

https://foursquare.com/v/schlossfreudenberg/4bdd4dee4ffaa593c6316ff7/photos

A rich English artist had built the large mansion around the turn of the twentieth century for his French girlfriend. When he fell on hard times and romantic difficulties, the German state of Hesse confiscated the estate. It eventually became a retreat center for Nazi SS officers. By the time the United Pentecostal Church acquired Schloss Freudenberg, the grand building on the Mountain of Joy (Freudenberg) showed her age and abuse. The Alvin Cobbs, the Wayne Nighs, and the Samuel Balcas did a wonderful job in converting the facility to house missionary personnel, the local church, and the Wiesbaden School of the Bible.

Wayne and Esther Nigh were on furlough when we arrived, but Sam and Pat Balca, the Nighs' furlough replacements for the German work, welcomed us and patiently helped us get settled in an apartment in Nordenstadt, a suburb of Wiesbaden.

Contrary to our hopes, Bev's health did not improve. The general practitioner that the Balcas used as a family doctor seemingly did not know anything about Crohn's disease. (In his defense, Crohn's disease was considered fairly rare at this time.) His suggestion that Bev drink a beer at least every other day to help her intestines showed that we were really in for some cultural shocks.

Eventually we were guided to Herr Professor Doctor "Schmidt." He was in charge of the Women's Clinic and head of the Gastroenterology Department at the medical school in the neighboring city of Mainz. I was impressed with his credentials. However, he read Bev's medical report from Dr. Berwald in St. Louis and, in his great wisdom, immediately decided she did not need the medications Dr. Berwald had prescribed. He soon hospitalized Bev in the Women's Clinic, which had been barracks for the German army during the last world war — and perhaps the first — and still looked like it.

When I first went to visit Bev, she was not in her room. I waited awhile, and she was wheeled in on a stretcher. One look at her gray skin frightened me. I thought she was dead! The doctors had used a rigid, eighteen-inch, metal sigmoidoscope to view Bev's lower bowel — without anesthesia. This test would be repeated again and again, apparently for the benefit of the medical students on their "grand rounds." If that was an example of modern German medicine, it wasn't for us!

After her experience with the great Herr Professor Doctor, Bev and I wrote off German medicine. The doctors had almost killed her once. We didn't want to give them another chance.

Aside from her health, life was good. We all really enjoyed Germany and had great hopes for the church. The children adjusted well. Krystin started giving English lessons to the German children in the neighborhood. Devon fit right in with blond hair and a tricycle. I continued in language school—shocked that my teacher, in accord with European custom, didn't shave under her arms—and I also taught in the Wiesbaden School of the Bible. Bev enjoyed going to the open market to buy fresh fruits and vegetables from the vendors, some of whom proudly told her their English was better than her German.

By this time, the Nighs had returned from furlough, and the local German assembly was growing.

Chapter 4

Bev: Living in Germany

The summer and fall of 1979 came and went, and I continued to learn to praise. By constant practice, praise became a continual attitude. I could smile and really be joyful even when I hurt. I could be thankful even when I could not get out of bed. I could praise when I could not keep food down. The circumstances had not changed one bit. I still woke up my husband by groaning at night. The pain was terrible. But I had changed.

The European family of God was a source of strength. Wayne and Esther Nigh, Samuel and Pat Balca, John and Darlene Goodwin, and Rich and Jeannie Collins were all neighboring missionaries who lent strength to our family. Terry Faulkner [now Sedra], a missionary helper at Schloss Freudenberg, was always willing to help.

I think the strength shown by all the missionary families can be best illustrated by our very close friends Rich and Jeannie Collins. One day, Dorsey called to say he was bringing company home. I was hurting so badly that I just didn't think I could act as if nothing was wrong.

Thank you, Ladies, for the washer, dryer, and refrigerator (not pictured).

I called Jeannie and at the sound of her comforting voice, I burst into tears with an "Oh, Jeannie!" Immediately she burst into tears with "Oh, Bev!" We both sobbed and sobbed over the long-distance phone lines.

Finally, she sniffed and said, "Bev, what are we crying about?" That struck me funny and I laughed and laughed. The crisis had passed, and a comforting friend had unknowingly given me the strength to jump the next hurdle.

Christmas in Germany was so much fun! However, I could not get away from the feeling that I had better be prepared for something. One night I had the dream about the plane again and told my husband, "Let's get everything ready. I'm going to have to go to the States soon."

We checked airline schedules. During our deputation travels, Pastor B. J. Robison—he and my husband were from the same home church in Modesto, California—had told us if we needed anything to let him know. We called, and he was wonderful. Yes, he had meant what he had offered, and he and his church would be glad to help.

The first week of January 1980, my father called from Portland. The doctors had operated on Mom and had given her just a few days to live. If I wanted to see her alive, I had better come home right away.

Thank God, He was in control. Everything was ready. I simply packed the suitcases and got on the plane. As I sat there, I looked at the woman on my left. She was wearing a brown, flowered silk dress. God never allows anything to come our way that He has not prepared us for!

On January 29, 1980, my mother passed away. Her last words were, "Oh, what a beautiful light!" Because I had learned to praise, her death did not devastate me.

After Mom's funeral, my aunt Toots, my sister-in-law Miriam, and I tried to organize things for Dad and Lurissa. All this time, I knew I was getting weaker. Toward the end of the job, my aunt and Miriam had to do most of it. I just could not seem to get it done.

Finally, things were as settled as the three of us could get them, and I felt it was time to go home to Europe. By now I could barely get through the day without going to bed, but I felt that if I could just get home and rest, I would be fine. I really missed my children and my husband, and I wanted to go home.

I was scheduled to leave at 8:00 Thursday morning. During the Wednesday night Bible study, I felt really sick and weak and spent most of the service in the restroom. On the way home, Dad talked me into going to the hospital for some pain pills to help me get back to

Germany. After an x-ray, I was told I had an intestinal blockage and would have to be admitted.

It was hard to praise that night. I missed Dorsey and the children so much, but it felt good to get a shot and have some relief from the pain.

A day or two after my admittance, a specialist came to tell me I had Crohn's disease (the common name for granulomatous colitis), that there was no cure, and that it would plague me all my life. An immediate operation was necessary to remove the blockage.

Soon after the operation, in which the doctor removed three feet of small intestine, I felt strong enough to wonder about this strange disease. I discovered that Crohn's disease creates small nodules or masses of inflamed tissue that penetrate the wall of the intestinal tract. It often skips around in the bowel, so it cannot be cured by surgery.

One doctor later told me that when he tells someone they have Crohn's, he feels as though he is sentencing a young person to a lifetime of pain and suffering from which there is no escape. He said, "I would rather tell someone they have cancer instead of Crohn's. At least with cancer they usually die."

Another doctor told me that if I had not had the surgery, within six months the buildup behind the blockage would have caused my intestine to rupture, after which I would have had about twenty-four hours to live. "Would the pain have been any worse?" I asked. The answer was no. Then I realized that had I gotten on the plane, I would have died, for I would not have gone back to a German doctor. I spent a long time thanking God for His mercy.

The time in the hospital was a time of drawing closer to God. About 5:00 AM every day we communed, and I can only describe these moments as sweet. One morning I awoke thinking of Psalm 121:1: "I will lift up mine eyes unto the hills, from whence cometh my help." David was talking not only about physical mountains but also about life's trials and experiences. Often we can look back at things we have had victory over and receive strength to face our next challenge. I decided I would never have a trial without putting another mountain in "my" mountain range!

The time in the hospital could have been devastating. Dad and Lurissa were trying to deal with their grief as well as comfort an older daughter and sister who really wanted to be in Germany. For a few days, I felt depressed about the whole situation.

Then praise once again entered the picture. After prayer one morning, I asked God to show me someone who could help me deal with the guilt and loneliness that I had due to being away from my husband and children.

Later, as I was walking down the hospital corridor, I met a little hunched-over woman. She looked to be in such bad shape that I asked if I could help her. We sat and she talked about her dead husband, children, sisters, mother, and father. I didn't say a lot, just listened. As she got up to leave, she patted my hand and said, "Thank you, dear. I feel so much better."

She felt better and I had learned a lesson—the all-important lesson of listening. I decided to use the time to develop this skill, and before long nurses, laboratory technicians, and housekeepers were spending lunch hours and breaks in my room talking—while I listened.

I made another life-changing decision about my lifestyle. I decided to really laugh at least once a day. Some days I had to look to find something funny, but an incident always showed up.

At the time I neither understand or cared that studies were being done to prove the very thing that I had discovered: People who laugh are healthier. I just knew I felt better.

Sometimes it was not a big thing. It could be something so small as a red-haired, freckled-faced child who would be giving his mother fits with his antics and then would look around her legs and grin at me. It could be something a nurse said or a comment I read, but something was always there to give me a physical, emotional, and even spiritual release.

Praise and laughter have turned out to be an unbeatable combination.

During this first hospital stay in the States, there were many setbacks—several blood transfusions and other things that kept going wrong. Finally, Dorsey decided he'd better come, and I was I ready to see him! As I said earlier, Terry Faulkner—now Terry Sedra and a missionary to Egypt—was working in Wiesbaden as a missionary helper and filling a multitude of roles as only she could. She kept Krystin and Devon while Dorsey came to get me. We will always be indebted to her.

My health improved, and three months after I left the hospital, I returned to Europe. I was feeling great and ready to do our part for revival in Europe. I got home in time for us to go to the European Conference in Dordrecht, Holland, where General Superintendent Nathaniel Urshan ordained Dorsey.

N. A. Urshan ordained Dorsey at the 1980 European Conference.

My husband and I had a burden for the city of Munich, and we made plans to move there. He went to Munich with the moving truck, and the children and I followed later in our Sheaves for Christ car. I was enjoying the lack of speed limits on the autobahn when construction narrowed the road. The car on my right swerved into my lane. As a reflex action, I twisted the wheel away from it, putting my car in the oncoming lane. At speeds of eighty to eighty-five miles per hour, there seemed to be no way to avoid death, but at the moment I felt the warmth of Someone's hand over mine. The car immediately straightened—in the correct lane. At the next rest stop, Krystin, Devon, and I had ourselves a praise service.

Munich was wonderful! I enrolled in a new language school. We started to make contacts. I was feeling good. It looked as if the battle was won.

In the midst of the good times, I told God I wanted a meek and quiet spirit. (See I Peter 3:4.) Not long after my prayer, I became ill again. This time I knew more of what was happening, and did I ever fight it! I took all the steps I knew for positive attitudes. I even told God that I really didn't care about a meek and quiet spirit, I just wanted to stay in Germany. However, I got weaker and sicker.

One of our neighbors was a doctor. Herr Doctor Mayr would come to my home at all hours of the day or night and give me injections of something so powerful that it was not on the US market. He would leave making comments under his breath about the American insurance system. If I hadn't been so sick, I probably would have been as vocal with my views on socialized medicine!

Eventually my health became so poor that Dorsey called Harry Scism, general director of Foreign Missions, for advice. A month to the day after we had dedicated our chapel in a glorious service—much like Solomon must have experienced at the dedication of the Temple—the Foreign Missions Administrative Committee decided we should return to the United States on an emergency medical furlough.

Chapter 5

Dorsey: Living Our Dream

We moved from Wiesbaden to Föching, a village south of Munich in Upper Bavaria, in June 1980, to pioneer a church in greater Munich. Harry Branding had helped found a church in Munich in the mid-1950s while he was pastoring Apostolic Pentecostal Church at Thirteenth and Gravois Streets in St. Louis. While some Charismatics and Trinitarian Pentecostal churches could be found in Munich, neither I nor any other United Pentecostal missionary could find any remnant of Brother Branding's group.

Nevertheless, we loved Bavaria! The Bavarians were friendlier than the Hessians of central Germany. The scenery was breathtakingly beautiful. The light rail ride into Munich was relaxing. The city of Munich was exciting—so full of history and bustling with people. I can't think of a thing we did not like about Bavaria.

Föching is a small village near Holzkirchen, just off the Munich-Salzburg autobahn as it curves to the east. Geranium-filled window boxes and murals depicting religious or folklore themes adorned the multi-level homes. And, as in many small German villages, farm animals lodged on the ground floor of the homes, bringing the country smells with them. We enjoyed walks through the village lanes.

We rented a row house, which corresponds to an American townhouse. Ours was sandwiched between two other units. It was newly constructed and much cheaper than anything we could have found closer to Munich. From the balcony of the children's bedrooms, we could see the German Alps in the distance. Herr Wimmer, our landlord, told me that had it been a few years earlier, he would not have rented to us as we were not Catholic.

We had about a twenty-minute ride to Krystin's school at the US army base. Unless the snow was too deep, Devon had an easy walk to his German kindergarten.

We were so happy and contended—except for Bev's health. Seeing her suffering—often writhing in pain—was a constant emotional torture. I knew we had been called to Germany and were in the will of God. Her illness was just another trial we had to bear up under and endure. Some missionaries suffer in hostile climates, and others endure oppressive government situations. Her disease was our cross. We had to be strong in the fight and expect God to give us the victory. After all, our list of German contacts was growing, and we were having some German prayer meetings. We were also having regular worship services with Jim and Lavonne Pugh and other Americans stationed in Munich.

While we were traveling on deputation or when we were visiting after Bev's first surgery, B. J. Robison introduced me to Paul E. Billheimer's book *Destined for the Throne*. The thin book's basic premise is that "the entire universe under the Son's regulation and control is being directed by God for one purpose—to prepare and train the Bride." In other words, everything that transpires or happens to us is designed by God to prepare us to rule and reign with Him. Life is simply boot camp for our eternal destiny. This book and its companion, *Don't Waste Your Sorrows,* jarred my thinking.

When coupled with Romans 8:28—"And we know that all things work together for good to them that love God, to them who are the called according to his purpose'"—these thoughts were revolutionary! This verse of Scripture does not state that all things are good. Some things simply are not good in themselves. Nevertheless, it emphatically declares that all things—including the bad things—can work for our good. For example, the crucifixion of Jesus purchased our salvation. Persecution scattered the early church and spread the gospel to the known world. And Paul's imprisonment gave him time to write the majority of the New Testament.

I still remember my disbelief as I first heard the late Ellston Hearn and his wife Donnie testify about the fireplace mantel that toppled and killed their infant daughter. As tragic as that situation was, it caused them to turn to God. Consequently, they, and those saved because of their witness, thanked God for using such a terrible accident for their good.

For years I had looked at Bev's disease as an enemy to our ministry, a demonic ploy to hinder our work for God.

It was at best a distraction that blurred my focus. After all, when Bev was unable to care for the kids or keep house and cook, I had to.

But could it be that Crohn's disease was a gift from God? (If so, I certainly did not like the packaging!) Could God be using it to develop and perfect us? Could it really work for our good? Could it be that I needed to embrace this trial as a welcomed friend? Could I really follow the apostle's advice in James 1:2-4:

> When all kinds of trials and temptation crowd into your lives, my brothers, don't resent them as intruders, but welcome them as friends! Realize that they come to test your faith and to produce in you the quality of endurance. But let the process go on until that endurance is fully developed, and you will find you have become men of mature character, men of integrity with no weak spots (Phillips).

Could I do that? No. Not on my own.

Bev's physical condition especially troubled me one day as I was showering. Why couldn't we get the victory over it? Prayer and fasting did not seem to help. I tried to follow the scriptural admonition to praise God *in spite of* the disease. That was my interpretation of "in every thing give thanks: for this is the will of God in Christ Jesus concerning you" (I Thessalonians 5:18). But that really wasn't helping. My praises seemed weighted with lead and fell from my tongue to the floor with a thud.

Nevertheless, somehow in that shower, God arrested my thoughts and made me see that He was really using Crohn's disease for our good. The disease was molding us, shaping us, refining us, and even purifying us. As I began to grasp the purpose of the disease, I became able to thank God *for* the disease and *for* the good that it was accomplishing in our lives. As I honestly praised Him for Crohn's disease, I felt Him cleansing my heart of the anger and resentment I had unconsciously carried. I left the shower washed inside and out.

On that day I discovered the great difference between I Thessalonians 5:18 and Ephesians 5:20, "Giving thanks always for all things unto God and the Father in the name of our Lord Jesus Christ." The difference is in the words *in* and *for*. It was only when I began to thank God *for* the disease that I really began to acknowledge His majesty and grace and allow Him to use His chosen tool to prepare us to rule and reign. Thanking *for* the disease is an affirmation of God's intrinsic goodness and recognizing—yes, even conceding—that He only wants what is best for us.

That was a life-changing experience!

Learning to praise *for* is vital if we are to experience victory. Psalm 68:1 says, "Let God arise, let his enemies be scattered: let them also that hate him flee before him." The natural question is: how do we let God arise and scatter His enemies? The answer is in Psalm 68:2–4: "As smoke is driven away, so drive them away: as wax melteth before the fire, so let the wicked perish at the presence of God. But let the righteous *be glad*; let them *rejoice before God*: yea, let them *exceedingly rejoice*. Sing unto God, *sing praises* to his name: *extol him* that rideth upon the heavens by his name JAH, and *rejoice before him*" (emphasis added). As we praise and worship Him, we release His power to work within and through us to accomplish His purpose in our lives and the lives of others. This was true when Jehoshaphat sent the choir out in front of the army to sing praises to God (II Chronicles 20). Likewise, it was true when Paul and Silas began to sing praises in prison (Acts 16).

In early January 1981, Bev and I were standing in the kitchen of our apartment. As we were talking, I heard God say, "You will be home by June." That didn't make any sense. We loved Germany, especially Bavaria, and had dedicated our lives to establish a church there. Bev's health was not great, but she didn't seem any worse than before. However, the voice was so strong that it may have been audible.

For the next couple of days, I walked through Gethsemane. All our married life had been geared to fulfilling our call to Germany. We had reduced our earthly possessions to what would fit in six fifty-gallon drums and a few suitcases before we left for Germany. We had committed to the long haul. We had no intention of returning to America except for furloughs and perhaps a family emergency involving our parents. We had gone to establish a church in Munich. The work was not done. Why was God sending us home when we were just starting?

I finally submitted my will to His without receiving any answers.

This photo adorned our PIM certificates.

Uncertain of what God was doing, we finished the work on the chapel in our basement. Missionaries Richard and Jeannie Collins and their daughters came over from Inzlingen, Germany, on the Swiss border, to dedicate the chapel on February 7, 1981. It was a glorious service. The Spirit of God was so heavy that it reminded me of the accounts of the dedication of Solomon's Temple and the fire that consumed Elijah's sacrifice on the altar. It seemed that God had placed His seal of approval on our efforts. We were excited about what God would accomplish in our chapel!

The next week I went to Wiesbaden to teach for a week in the Bible school. When I returned home, Bev had taken a drastic turn for the worse. She could hardly get out of bed. Her pain was unbearable.

I found an American-trained, English-speaking gastroenterologist in downtown Munich. He examined Bev and concluded that the Crohn's had constricted her rectum to the width of a pencil. His only prescription was for her to take seven enemas a day. She took one. The pain so drastically increased that the children asked, "Daddy, is Momma going to die?" I didn't know. I was frightened too.

I called Harry Scism, the general director of Foreign Missions, and explained the situation. He did not make a snap decision but instead said, "Let's pray about it.'" A week later, a month to the day of our chapel dedication, Edwin Judd, the secretary of Foreign Missions, called and said the Foreign Missions Administrative Committee had given us an emergency medical furlough and we should return to the United States as soon as possible.

I did not want to return to the US. However, I had heard the voice of God and knew this was somehow a part of His plan. Again, He was using Bev's Crohn's disease to accomplish His will in our lives. This knowledge granted me some form of stability in a dream world that had changed to a nightmare.

Missionary Carol Rash and her daughter Darla came over from Vienna, Austria, to join LaVonne and LaDusta Pugh, Americans living in Munich, in helping us pack. Bev told them what to pack, and they did the work. Missionaries Richard Collins and John Goodwin helped me load the truck and move our belongings to the Schloss in Wiesbaden.

As we were loading the truck, Herr Wimmer, our landlord, came over, asking if someone could explain a tract I had given him. Brother Collins took time to talk to him.

Since it was God's will for us to leave, where was the person who was supposed to take our place? God had told Bev that He had called someone, but he had *refused* to go. Our hearts ached because of our shattered dreams. Knowing souls might never hear the gospel because someone refused to take our place left us confused, frustrated, and angry. How could that person be so stupid as to refuse to go to Bavaria?

Chapter 6

Bev: From Germany to St. Louis

We spent the night before leaving Germany at the Mannheim home of missionaries John and Darlene Goodwin. Everyone except me went on to service. I walked the floor, wondering how I could ever make a sixteen-hour airplane journey with two small children. At 9:00 I suddenly got relief! It was instantaneous. I did not ask why. I simply thanked God.

We flew into San Francisco, and later went to the church in El Sobrante, California, pastored by B. J. Robison. Elderly Sister Evans, the former pastor's widow, came over to me and asked what had happened to me on Wednesday at 2:00 West Coast time. She said that she had been awakened with a tremendous burden and had spent hours interceding for me. I suddenly realized who had touched God for me the night before. God was still controlling things!

Burk Family, 1981, shortly after returning from Germany

After a medical examination in Portland, Oregon, the doctors decided I should be given a colostomy. This surgical procedure involves rerouting the intestines to end at an opening (an ostomy) in the abdominal wall, thus bypassing the rectum. I opposed this surgery with all I had. *No way* would I wear a bag to catch the waste. NO WAY!

At the same time, the Foreign Missions Board wisely decided not to reappoint us to Germany. Until my health improved, they knew that Dorsey needed to stay close to me and not travel all over the country on deputation. I loved Germany. I loved the people and felt sick about not returning. But it really felt wonderful to know my disease would be treated in the United States. We knew that the board's decision was in the will of God.

Although we experienced great relief over not going back to Europe until my health improved, we did not know what we were to do next. The next ten months were a struggle.

My hardest times were at night. I had a recurring dream that involved a very elderly Bavarian woman whom we had befriended. She was one of the sweetest women I had ever met. A dedicated Catholic, she walked to mass every day at 6:00 AM—rain, snow, sleet, or hail.

In my dream, Tanta Anna was walking down the street to Mass, looking over her shoulder at me with such hunger and longing that I couldn't stand the pain. I would start beating the glass on the patio window, yelling at the top of my voice, "Tanta Anna, that's not right! Come back! My German is good enough to explain salvation to you now! PLEASE COME BACK!" And she would continue walking, looking back at me with that haunting hunger. She couldn't hear me. The glass was too thick.

We had apparently done what God had sent us to Bavaria to do. Our time was finished. God had spoken, and there was no doubt. But no one had come to take our place, and souls were still dying. Sometimes it was more of a burden than I could bear.

Bev, 1991. This is Dorsey's favorite photo.

Why hadn't God allowed us to stay? We loved — and still love — Germany with the love of a parent and a child. We hadn't wanted to come home. Why hadn't God given Crohn's to someone else who didn't want to go and do His work? It was a hard time.

In October I decided the quality of life I was enduring could not be worse than living with a colostomy. I could not go anywhere unless a bathroom was near—which excluded many shopping malls! So in early November, I had the necessary surgery. Two weeks later I had another surgery to remove yet another intestinal blockage.

After the first surgery, I was told the doctor had planned to remove the rectal stump, thus making the colostomy permanent. But due to the tremendous inflammation, they decided to wait. During the second surgery, they saw such improvement that they again decided not to remove that area. They did not understand what was happening, but I did. God had promised complete healing!

In December Harry Scism called the hospital room to talk to Dorsey. The Foreign Missions workload at World Evangelism Center had grown to the point that they need someone to help, primarily with publications—promotional items such as the *Global Witness* (now called *OnSite*) and training materials for use in the foreign Bible schools. Would Dorsey be interested? There was much rejoicing that day! God was giving us another area of foreign missions in which to serve!

After our move back to St. Louis, my health became worse and then tolerable—only to revert to worse. It was back and forth: n the hospital for tests; out for a few weeks; back in for more tests. In one year, I was in the hospital seven times. I knew there was a blockage, but the tests did not show it.

During the winter of 1983, I was reading my Bible when the words of Isaiah 30:19-21 seemed to stand out from the biblical text.

> For the people shall dwell in Zion at Jerusalem: thou shalt weep no more: he will be very gracious unto thee at the voice of thy cry; when he shall hear it, he will answer thee. And though the Lord give you the bread of adversity, and the water of affliction, yet shall not thy teachers be removed into a corner any more, but thine eyes shall see thy teachers: and thine ears shall hear a word behind thee, saying, This is the way, walk ye in it, when ye turn to the right hand, and when ye turn to the left.

I knew my experience with Crohn's was almost over.

In March 1983, my doctor came running into my hospital room. The blockage had been found. Surgery was quickly scheduled, and in the preoperative discussion, Dr. David Berwald mentioned that he would probably take out the rectal stump.

The first thing I remember after surgery was seeing my husband beside my bed having a terrible time sitting still. As soon as he knew I was awake, he said, "They can't find any Crohn's!"

"That's nice," I replied and went back to sleep. As soon as I came fully awake, I immediately remembered what Dorsey had said. There was no visible Crohn's!

The next day the doctor told me there had been a blockage caused by a slipped staple from a previous operation. Then he said the words I'd been waiting so long to hear: "We can't find any Crohn's." I started crying and asking him to repeat himself—to please say it one more time!

When was I healed? I don't know—possibly when Jack Yonts or C. M. Becton stopped work to come to my home and anoint me. Or it could have been one of the many times that Pastor Guy Roam prayed for me. Or possibly it happened when some saint somewhere around the world touched God's throne on my behalf.

Chapter 7

Dorsey: The Road Gets Rougher

We rejoiced in Bev's freedom from Crohn's disease. But our rejoicing lasted only for a year or so at the most. It wasn't long until the symptoms recurred.

She was hospitalized twice in 1985, twice in 1986 (including Christmas), twice in 1987, once in 1988, once in 1989, once in 1990 (including her birthday), and once in 1991. Each time the blocked segment of intestine had to be surgically removed and the remaining pieces stitched together.

By now the children were old enough to understand more fully the extent of Bev's illness. Each one reacted to the bouts of sickness in his or her own way. Krystin, the older, usually assumed more responsibilities around the house. Devon, the younger, internalized his feelings and fears and sought refuge in his room. It shocked me to realize that his mother had seen sick his whole life. It was difficult to make plans as a family, for we never knew when Bev would be rushed to the emergency room and hospitalized again.

During such times, I developed empathy for single parents. It is difficult being dad, mom, housekeeper, gardener, taxi driver, cook, chef, and all the other roles parents must play. (Thankfully Krystin was able to care for her hair. Early on that had been a hassle for both of us. Usually some lady at church would have pity on her and recomb my best efforts.) Somehow we managed to survive—thanks to a large extent to the New Life family that frequently sent food when Bev was hospitalized—and thanks also to frozen potpies.

Frozen potpies were my normal solution to dinner. They were quick; they were cheap; and they came in a variety of flavors. However, the mere mention of potpies today causes Krystin and Devon—and me—to gag. I can't remember the last time we had one of those frozen entrées at our house.

During one of the surgeries, Dr. Berwald had to move the ostomy from Bev's left side to the right, as the shortened bowel would not stretch to the old opening. Before discharging her, he explained I would need to help her care for the old site until it had healed. I had seen stapled incisions over and over and thought, *No big deal.* When he called me over, I went confidently to the bed so he could show me what to do.

What he showed me was not a nicely stapled incision. Instead it was a gaping hole, about an inch and a quarter in diameter and an inch or so deep, showing layer after layer of tissue: skin, muscle, and fat. The hole was stitched at the bottom, so it could heal from the bottom up. While I did not have the strongest stomach in the world, incisions no longer bothered me. However, I was not prepared for this sight. My world spun around, and I thought I was headed for the floor.

The doctor was wrong. Bev did not need my help. She did an excellent job of cleaning her own wound and bandaging it herself. She knew she could do that easier than lifting me off the floor or cleaning up after me.

Coming from a long line of educators—our daughter is the sixth generation on Bev's side of the family—Bev always took great interest in our children's education, frequently volunteering at their school. Her natural abilities impressed the principal and counselor, both of whom urged her to complete her degree in education. The principal then recommended Bev for a teacher's aide position. Bev took the position of teaching remedial reading on a one-on-one basis for a year and discovered that she enjoyed having her own classroom.

Bev graduated from Missouri Baptist College with a BSE in Education.

With my encouragement and that of teaching professionals, Bev enrolled at Missouri Baptist College, which accepted many of her credits from Conquerors Bible College. Consequently, the late 1980s were even more trying for Bev as she was completing her degree in elementary education while coping with her illness. Nevertheless, she graduated in April 1989 with a Bachelor of Science in Education. She missed graduating *cum laude* by one-hundredth of a point, because her credits from CBC had to be factored in. (She readily admitted that she had *fun* in Bible school.)

We all were proud of her! Her graduation testified to Bev's tenacity and spirit. Her grit and determination inspired many. The World Evangelism Center executive wives marked the occasion by honoring her at a graduation party hosted by Margie Becton. The Foreign Missions secretaries also gave her a luncheon.

Throughout Bev's illness, the Foreign Missions Division was very supportive. Harry Scism, the other executives, and the staff members were very understanding when family situations demanded a flexible work schedule. We are thankful for our continued involvement in foreign missions.

I enjoyed my job with Foreign Missions, especially the creative challenges it posed in editing and designing *World Harvest Today* magazine and designing the General Conference displays. Although I tried to restrict the number of days I was out of the office, I also enjoyed traveling to present the blessing of Faith Promise giving. Working in the division gave us a broader perspective of missions than we had had while in Europe. However, working so closely with the missionaries produced its own set of problems.

While we were physically in St. Louis, our hearts remained in Europe. Perhaps we were like the pouty boy in church who said, "I'm sitting down, but on the inside I'm still standing up!" We knew God had orchestrated our return to the US. We knew that physically Bev needed the medical attention she was getting. We knew God had given us a place to work in missions. Yet we also knew we were so close to dreams but still so far away.

One of the hardest things I did during those early years following our return was to go to a missionary service. To keep my heart from breaking, I steeled myself and became analytical: *His presentation would have been better if he had changed the progression of the slides. He should have cut out about fifteen minutes; he lost the congregation when he kept talking about _____. He needs to emphasize _____. He needs to do something, so I don't hurt so much!*

The general conference Foreign Missions services were even worse. I was often a part of the committee planning the service and had responsibilities during the service itself. However, when it came time for the call for laborers at the end, it was only God and me. He knew that as a child and young teen, I had never wanted to be a minister, let alone a missionary. Yet He had placed the call on our lives. He knew we were willing to go. And we knew He had brought us home in His will. So why did it hurt so much? Was Bev's ongoing physical struggle the result of some rebellion on my part? Was I wrong to hope that someday she would be well and that we could return to Germany?

I had very few answers. I just knew that going to a missionary service cut like a knife. But you can't teach your children to love missions and to dedicate their lives to God's will by avoiding missionary services. Sometimes you just bear the pain.

In early 1992, Bev developed another blockage. However, as we were in the middle of planning our daughter's wedding, she told the doctor she could not have surgery until after the wedding in June. By then the doctors were accustomed to Bev consulting her calendar before scheduling surgeries or tests and simply saying, "I just don't have time now. It will have to wait until after _____." Through the years she has somehow endured the pain, consistently resisting the disease's domination of her life.

Krystin became Mrs. Kent Noel Carlson on June 20, 1992, at New Life Center, Bridgeton, MO. Pastor Jim Roam and Grandpa Sponsler officiated.

So, in late June, about a week after Krystin became Mrs. Kent Noel Carlson on June 20, 1992, Dr. Berwald performed what we had expected to be "another routine intestinal resection." Bev had already had so many that we had lost count. However, the recurrence of Crohn's had affected a greater area of the bowel than he realized. Consequently, he removed a large portion of her small intestine, leaving only about six feet. (Her entire colon had been removed in several pervious resections.) The doctors assured us that the remaining intestine would adapt within six months, and she would be able to absorb enough nutrients to function normally. They also told us that for some inexplicable reason, symptoms of Crohn's disease often just disappear when the intestine is reduced to such a small amount.

She was sent home a few days after the surgery. Her ostomy continued to put out waste unabatedly. She was nauseated, unable to eat, and simply wanted to sleep. Two or three days later I suddenly realized the extent of her listlessness and rushed her back to the hospital. Her blood pressure was 60/40. She was in hypo-volumetric shock, a condition produced by severe dehydration.

From that point on, Bev began a downward spiral. The battle was no longer with Crohn's disease but with the side effects caused by the ravages of the illness.

Her intestine did not adapt as the doctors had expected. Everything she ate rushed through her limited digestive tract. Although she had a voracious appetite and ate constantly, she continued to lose weight. In reality, she was starving to death because her body could not absorb the nutrients that ever so quickly filled her ostomy bag. Her weight dropped from 135 to 86 pounds.

To compensate for her lack of intestinal function, a feeding tube was inserted into her stomach, and she "fed" herself predigested food and Pedialyte with a large syringe through the tube. That was followed by a series of permanent IV lines and porta-caths implanted in her shoulders or arms leading directly to the heart. These permanent IV lines, aka "central lines," allowed her to hook up to large, intravenous feeding bags that contained all the nutrients a person needs to maintain health. In this way she received nourishment while she slept at night in her own bed. This process is called total parenteral nutrition (TPN) or hyperalimentation.

The downside of this procedure is that the IV lines are prone to infections. Time and time again the catheters became infected, allowing bacteria to enter the bloodstream, a condition known as sepsis. The old IV line would have to be removed and a new one surgically implanted. Along with the new line, she received large doses of strong antibiotics.

She was in the hospital from December 1992 through January 1993 with another bout of sepsis. Staph infection invaded her bloodstream. An infectious disease doctor — who seemed to be at the top of the medical pecking order — was called in on the case. He postured and made various demands of the staff. The doctors kowtowed to his remedy. The nurses quaked in his wake. He was a formidable personality.

At the same time, the Dillard's department store clearance center in downtown St. Louis was having a sale. The clearance center's prices were normally 75 percent off the original price. This sale was an additional 50 percent off the discounted price. Bev quickly understood this meant everything was only 12.5 percent of the normal retail price—or 87.5 percent off. She just had to get down there! She had, after all, lost almost fifty pounds, and none of her clothes fit.

The infectious disease doctor was in shock when Bev asked for a pass to go shopping. Of course, she could not go! However, "Dr. God`" had not dealt with my wife. Taking her cue from the widow in the New Testament story of the unjust judge, she badgered the doctor until he relented. Nevertheless, to save face, he demanded that she use a wheelchair.

In a few hours she returned to the hospital laden with a new wardrobe and praising God for His merciful bounty—and even for allowing us to surprise Steve and Erma Judd, who are like family, at Dillards. As the weeks passed, she and "Dr. God" developed quite a rapport. We were sorry when he moved on to another hospital.

In February 1993 I flew to North Dakota to hold a series of meetings promoting Faith Promise throughout the district. When I arrived, I had a message to call home. After I had left that morning, Bev's IV line had sprung a leak and had to be replaced immediately. By the time I called, the procedure had already taken place. She assured me she was fine and at home.

No one realized at that time that the surgeon in the emergency room had inserted the catheter too close to her heart. The constant propulsion from the nightly feedings damaged the right atrium wall of her heart.

A few weeks later Bev began to run a 103-degree fever. She lived on aspirin and Tylenol and continued to teach fifth grade at the public elementary school near our home. She often had difficulty focusing on a thought and appeared confused. Finally, the principal, who was also a dear friend, insisted she see the school nurse. Bev could no longer hide the raging fever.

Her fever continued to climb after she was hospitalized. Severe chills would seize her body, and she would shake the heavy hospital bed as she shivered. Then the fever would begin to spike, with each spike getting a little higher until they were consistently over 106 degrees.

To combat Bev's chills, the nurses would wrap her in blankets heated in the autoclave. Then as the fever spiked, they would remove the blanket and pack her with ice. One time the nurse left the warm blankets and simply added ice. I thought, *Boy, this is really crazy.*

It was quite apparent that the medical staff did not know what to do. The doctors consulted and called in more specialists. They x-rayed and tested. They didn't know what to say, so they offered no words of comfort to allay my fears. They knew Bev had an infection raging in her body. However, isolating it and treating it remained elusive even for "Dr. God." As the days turned to multiple weeks, the nurses began to avoid looking me in the eye.

The prolonged infection and high fevers were taking their toll. Bev slept more and more and grew weaker and weaker. Pastor Jerry Jones asked the congregation to pray but not to visit. (Visitation was restricted to fellow ministers. I still remember the shocked expression on Bob and Susan Fuller's faces when the hospital bed moved because of Bev's violent chills.) Sister Becton later said the only question in her mind was whether the body would be buried in St. Louis or taken back to Oregon.

Naturally, I was worried and frustrated. Medical science was proving again that it is only a "practice." I was also irritated because I knew God could heal Bev. But He wouldn't. I found myself growing hard and bitter.

My responsibilities at the Foreign Missions Division were probably the only thing that kept me sane. Christian Hospital Northwest was located between our house and World Evangelism Center. I would stop by the hospital on my way to work in the mornings and then return to the hospital at noon and after work. The work made me focus on the matters at hand instead of thinking about Bev and what might lie ahead.

One night I was especially depressed. It hurt to watch Bev shiver with chills and then bake with fever. I was tired of the nurses and doctors refusing to look at me. I was also weary of the pity in their eyes when they thought I wasn't looking. Medical science couldn't do anything, and God wouldn't. I went home and tried to pray, but my fear and anger at God hindered me. I had forgotten the lesson about praising God *for* all things.

The ringing of the telephone aroused my attention. On the other end was Darry Crossley, a longtime friend and a missionary on deputation. He was simply calling to see how things were going and to say that he cared. Something about his call helped me to refocus and break through the bitterness and anger that I harbored. It felt so good to repent and feel the Holy Ghost cleanse away the filth that had accumulated in my heart. It took awhile, but as I began to praise God *for* His goodness and kindness, I received peace that I needed.

Within days, the doctors pinpointed Bev's problem. A trans-esophageal echocardiogram (TEE) showed bacteria growing like seaweed *inside* her heart. When the bacteria would break off from the main mass and enter the bloodstream, the fever would spike, and the body's defenses would take over. The only solution was open-heart surgery to literally excise the bacteria.

The surgery was set for April 7, 1993. Although I felt peaceful about the surgery and knew that everything would be okay, I didn't know what that meant. I only knew that I had committed my wife to God's care. He would either guide the surgeon's hands and let her live, or He would give me the strength to endure the loss. Before I left my office on April 6, I laid an envelope addressed to Edwin Judd ("Pappaw" to my kids) on my desk. Inside was an outline for the funeral service should the operation fail. I had faced our mortality and still could praise God *for* knowing what was best.

The surgical waiting room looked like a church social as friends and family gathered to lend their support. Bev's missionary brother had flown in from Ecuador. Her father and stepmother were already in town. Friends came from Ohio, Indiana, and Tennessee to join local friends, including those from World Evangelism Center. Large gift baskets of goodies made the place feel festive, and light-hearted conversation masked some of the underlying tension.

After a few hours, the nurse practitioner came to give us a report. The doctors had expected the bacteria to be growing on one of the heart valves and were prepared to replace it. However, when they opened the heart, they discovered that the bacterial growth was on the wall of the right atrium where propulsion from the IV catheter had bruised the tissue. The good news was the valve would not have to be replaced then. The bad news was the bacterial mass was much greater than they had anticipated.

After a few more hours, the surgeon came to assure us that everything was all right. He had excised the damaged area, removed all the bacteria, and cleansed the heart. Bev would spend the next day or two in ICU and then be transferred to her own room. He expected her to make a full recovery from the heart surgery—although he said the heart valve would have to be replaced within five years because of her congenital heart murmur.

Sometime later, Dr. Berwald saw the surgeon and complimented him on his fine work. However, Dr. Richard Shaw replied that it was not his skill but the prayers of the thirty-some people in the waiting room that made the difference.

Chapter 8

Bev: The Promise

God never leaves an unplugged hole in our heart! Our time as on-the-field missionaries was finished, and we were settled in St. Louis. My health was okay—well, kind of okay—and I was looking for something to do.

I had always volunteered at the elementary schools my children attended, and went to see, once again, where I could be used. Being from a family of teachers, I had cut my teeth on textbooks. Many summer vacations were spent helping my dad teach summer school. It was a natural place to be.

Imagine my shock when Phyllis Stoecklein, the school's principal, said, "Bev, we don't want you here." I didn't know educators ever turned down anything free! However, Phyllis went on, "We need you in our classrooms. Go back and get your degree." What a ridiculous idea! It seemed ludicrous that a person with my health record would even try a new career, let alone one that required several years of college.

Totally out of the question—wasn't it. Well, how would I ever know if I could handle a forty-plus-hour-a-week if I didn't try it? I filled out an application to be a teacher's assistant and within a month had an interview.

Bev leading her class in the school's annual Halloween parade.

Three times in my life I have had an instant feeling of belonging. Once was as we got off the plane to join the Bible school staff in Kingston, Jamaica; the second was when we drove into the city limits of Munich, West Germany; and the third was walking down the steps at Airport Elementary School. I knew this would be a wonderful experience.

And I was right. I got a surge of energy when I walked into a classroom. It was a constant challenge to try to instill a concept in a child who often wasn't very interested in having it instilled. I didn't think I could be happier.

After two years of assisting, I decided to quit my job, go back to college full time, and get my teacher's certificate. Let's let those three years pass with the comment that my grade point average in Bible school was 2.5, or C, while my Missouri Baptist College GPA was 3.97. Suffice it to say, my time at Conquerors Bible College was a lot more interesting.

Eventually, I was hired by a wonderful principal to teach fourth grade. My team partner had a similar teaching style, so we got along tremendously well. Thanksgiving came while we studied the Pilgrims. Our classrooms became log cabins. Math time was spent estimating how many dips in wax it took to make a candle. In Social Studies we planned hunting trips. Rag dolls were made and written about. We concluded the unit with a Pilgrim's feast, complete with original recipes. We worked very hard, but we had energetic, alive classrooms. I was fulfilled and extremely content.

At home my children were growing up. Krystin had begun to date, and before long, she met Mr. Right in the form of a young Minnesotan named Kent Carlson. Kent fit right into the family—in fact, so much so that Krystin told another young lady, "Make sure your parents like your husband, but not too much, or they will never side with you in a fight!"

Krystin and Kent now live in South Bend, Indiana. She started out as a special education teacher, but later became the principal of the school district's public Montessori school, one of very few public Montessori schools in the nation. Kent worked as a customer service supervisor for a national company specializing in small motorized tools. Unfortunately, Krystin developed several serious health issues and went on full-time disability. When her health further declined, Kent quit his job to become her full-time caregiver. Maybe someday they will write their own story of miracles.

After the wedding, I had another surgery, but it was nothing to be upset about. It was just another intestinal resection. However, this time I didn't recover as fast as previously. I spent more time in bed, but it didn't help. The crisis came when I tried to turn over and couldn't. I had to kind of flop and let the momentum from my arms pull me on over. I was suffering from hypo-volumetric shock, which is extreme dehydration. A very difficult time began.

Often, when people go through a very hard physical time, they simply don't remember it. God, in His wisdom, has created the human mind so that it simply blocks out what it can't handle. The only things I recall about the following year are memories that look like still photos. I can remember scenes but not sequences.

I do know I taught fifth grade, but I was so sick that I honestly don't remember enjoying it. I remember knowing a few facts in a meeting but being unable to process them. It was as if they were floating just out of reach. It was frustrating. I simply couldn't think.

I continued to teach, but it soon became obvious to everyone that something was seriously wrong. I thought I was doing fairly well until one day I found myself giving incorrect answers to the students. I became very frightened. However, I continued to teach.

IVs kept me alive. At night I would hook myself up to a pump and infuse the nutrition I would need for the next day. It was a workable situation except for the catheter that had been inserted insert through the chest wall and into one of the main veins of the body kept getting infected, requiring another round of potent antibiotics. I began to panic whenever I ran a fever.

One time when Dorsey was out of town, I looked down to find something wet on my dress. After further investigation, I realized there was a hole in the tubing that connected to the IV. I was immediately sent to the hospital for a line replacement.

The ER doctor replaced the line, but unbeknownst to any of us, he placed it too close to the heart. Things went from bad to worse. I continued to teach but started having chills. I would be talking to the kids and start shaking — there would be no way to control or avoid it.

I was so thirsty all the time. I constantly drank, but there was no relief from the terrible thirst.

By this time, I was taking four to six non-aspirin pain relievers per hour but was still suffering all the symptoms. As I knew I would not have a job the following year if I missed any more work, I did my best to hide the problems. In my very muddled thinking, I assumed the symptoms would just go away.

One day the school secretary came into my classroom and said that Susan, my principal, wanted to see me immediately. When I walked into the office, the school nurse took my temperature and pulse and pronounced me sick. Dorsey was called, and I was sent home.

Instead of home, however, I soon found myself in the hospital. I can remember the doctor sitting in a chair commenting, "Um, I've never seen anyone survive such a low potassium level." That spoke faith to my heart!

The other scene that is engraved in my memory is the chills. I would get so cold that the nurse would cover me with several heated blankets, and someone else would spoon-feed me with hot tea. I would shake so badly that the hospital bed would move.

There were still humorous things that happened. I had a roommate who had Alzheimer's disease. I thought I had established somewhat of a rapport with her — that is, until she decided to go home.

The hospital staff had to put her in restraints because she couldn't walk, but that didn't keep her from trying. She would wriggle out of the restraints and try to take off again. Finally, a staff member sat and watched her, but she would simply wait until the person's head was turned and wriggle out of those restraints faster than could be imagined.

Security guards were finally brought in. The room was full of what she thought were firemen. The little lady started yelling, "Don't you scratch that dining suite. It's expensive. I'll sue you!"

It was later that night. I was very sick and tired, and thought I might get some sleep if I could calm her down. I leaned over and said, "Do you remember me? I'm Bev. We're friends."

My "friend`" looked at me and said, "YOU HUSH! If I want to hear from you, I'll tell you!" There may have been many times when others have wanted to say the same thing to me, but she just came right out with it. I just said okay and covered my head with a pillow.

I can also remember the many friends and family members who came from so many places to be with us. Although at some level, I appreciated their concern, I know that my family appreciated it more.

Serious illness is a very strange thing. The patient, in some respects, has the easier role to play. She is fighting for her life or fighting against the illness, but at least she is actively doing something. The family has to sit and just watch. My illness has made me very sympathetic toward those who have sit on the sidelines. They need prayer too.

One of the last "still pictures`" I remember is a scene as I was going to the operating room. (I must have been concerned about whether I would survive or not, although I can't remember the emotion.) I remember looking up and seeing Jim Stark, pastor of Calvary Apostolic Church in Columbus, Ohio. I don't remember him saying anything, but when he looked at me, I knew that everything would be fine. From then on, I began to look on this as more of an adventure than a burden.

I woke up in a very strange place. I can remember thinking, *WOW! I've never been hooked up to this many machines before.* I could see my family at a window and wanted to wave, but I was just too tired.

It was a very long recovery. I knew that I would not be able to teach the following year, but I wanted to talk to Susan in person before I tendered my resignation. However, one day I got a phone call. It was Susan, who said, "Due to your absenteeism, the district has decided not to renew your contract." Just like that. Boom! I was fired!

It was hard to take, but I had not earned tenure, so my job had no protection. I loved teaching and had hoped to be able to take a leave of absence instead of total job loss.

That night was pretty long. I cried many tears. However, I decided a couple of things: (1) If I ever fired someone, it would be face-to-face and not over a telephone. (2) I didn't like Dorsey traveling by himself as much as he had been. If I didn't have a forty-hour-per-week job, I could be free to travel with him. I began to feel more positive.

I will probably always miss not having my own classroom. I fit there. I belonged there. In counselor's jargon, it was my comfort zone. The first September I did not teach was really rough. I stood in front of a school supply display at a drugstore and realized that no one would be coming to fill a list I had sent—and promptly burst into tears. All the other customers probably thought it was the price of the pencils that had me upset, but there was a huge hole in my life.

But God is not the God of holes. First, as I regained my strength, I traveled with Dorsey. Then Word Aflame

Publications asked that I do some freelance writing and proofreading for Sunday school materials, and I did that as needed. And I got stronger.

Another important event happened during this recuperation time. I had a very dear friend who was a first-grade teacher in my school. Her twenty-five-year-old daughter had a routine dental procedure. However, something was not done properly, and this young lady developed endocarditis. (Endocarditis is an infection of the inner lining of the heart chambers and valves.) It was the very same thing that I had had, but she died—one month before her wedding.

I went to the funeral. As I was sitting, almost feeling guilty I had survived, I heard God speak to my heart. My work wasn't finished. I had more things to do and more adventures to pursue. It was a very sobering time.

Each Christian has to have times of taking a good, long look at his or her own life. Each one must assess where he has been and where he is going. This was one of those times for me. As I sat in that funeral, I realized that education had become my all-consuming force. I loved God, but my mind and energy were seldom on Him. Being an educator had become the center of my life. God, in His goodness, had refocused my priorities.

I gained strength but not weight. Even the total parenteral nutrition (TPN) could not seem to get my weight over 100 pounds. Shopping for clothes was a horror. I couldn't find anything to fit, much less something I liked!

Finally, my gastroenterologist suggested that we investigate intestinal transplants. Talk about a new adventure! Intestinal transplants were experimental and, at that stage, not very successful. However, at that point, it seemed the only door open.

I was shocked when my insurance approved the transplant application—in Wisconsin. I filled out what seemed to be reams of papers, sent them to the University of Wisconsin in Madison, and waited.

A date was set for Dorsey and me to go up for an interview. After the flight and a long sojourn in the waiting room, we were finally ushered into the doctor's office. The interview went something like this:

"Do you want a transplant?" Well, the answer was no. I had done research and knew having a transplant would be very involved, tedious, and would change the rest of my life. It meant I would be spending my life on pills—some of which I already had had bad reactions to. Want this operation? No, thanks! But it seemed the only way.

"Okay," was the esteemed doctor's reply. "You are on the list." Just like that! I started feeling very apprehensive. Something wasn't right; I just didn't know what. This feeling was reinforced when I mentioned my reaction to steroids. When I take them, I get violent. "Don't worry," I was assured, "we will pad your room."

Whoa! The red flags that had gone up during the interview started waving ferociously. The attitude of the transplant office seemed to be simply that they wanted another body to perform a transplant on. I don't think they ever saw me as an individual, and it bothered me that there was no testing. There was nothing to indicate they would be interested in my family unit and a transplant's effect on them.

The mileage between my home and the hospital bothered me. What if my body started rejecting? The only answer I could get was, "Well, most people move here." That wasn't an option.

After talking about the situation, Dorsey and I decided to go ahead, because it seemed the only door available. However, I later told Jerry Jones, my pastor at New Life Center, that I would never have the transplant. That statement did not represent a bad attitude, just a knowledge that I would never have one.

By this time, I had started substitute teaching. I really enjoyed the challenge. It kept me somewhat involved in education. If I physically couldn't work, I simply didn't take the job. God had once again plugged the hole.

Dorsey petitioned the insurance company on my behalf to have the transplant at Barnes-Jewish Hospital in St. Louis. It is known nationwide as a wonderful teaching hospital, and it was close to home. The insurance company agreed, and the process began again.

My experience at Barnes was very different than what I went through in Wisconsin. I underwent three days of testing, including heart tests, psychological and sociological tests, and testing of my family. They wanted to see if I would have the support at home to have a successful transplant.

One of the social workers who interviewed us asked about a support system. I began to tell her about two ladies who had come over, cleaned my house, and fixed dinner for three days. I had not asked for help; they had talked among themselves and decided that I would be very tired and would not feel like keeping up with my work at home. That was an example of *my* support system.

The social worker made an interesting statement. She said that, if possible, Barnes prefers to perform a transplant on someone with a deep religious faith. People who have a walk with God recover much faster and do not reject their new organ as much as those without it.

All the testing was finally over. However, the doctors thought there was one more thing they could try. It involved drinking only a certain liquid. When I asked what it tasted like, the subject was always changed. I got the feeling that I wasn't going to enjoy this much.

For this last attempt to avoid a transplant, I was admitted to Barnes-Jewish Hospital. The doctors never did give me the liquids because my intestines started working enough to avoid the entire procedure. They were flabbergasted, but I wasn't. I had known that I would never have the transplant.

On the home front, Devon had grown into a wonderful young man. He had decided not to serve Christ, and that broke our heart, but he did love us. He began dating Christina O'Brien, a beautiful young lady he had met at high school. Her mother had come from Hong Kong, and Christina's Asian background gave our family a new dimension. They were married August 2, 1997, in a beautiful service at New Life Center. Christina later received the Holy Ghost and was baptized by Pastor Jerry Jones.

During this time, Thetus Tenney was asked to begin the World Network of Prayer (WNOP). Part of the concept was to have a toll-free number with a volunteer available for prayer. It was a bold, new idea, and I was honored to be a part of it.

In 1997, the first Summons to Sacrifice prayer conference was held at New Life Center, Bridgeton,

From left to right: Pappaw and Granny Judd, George and Virginia Sponsler, Christina and Devon, Bev and Dorsey Burk

Missouri. I was a volunteer, but more important, I was a participant. The church was packed, and God's Spirit was very strong.

I don't know exactly what happened to my spiritual being, but something changed during that meeting. I moved into a new dimension, and it was totally life changing. God became more than just my God. He became my friend, the kind of friend I could enjoy talking to over a cup of coffee, the kind of friend who was interested in the small details of my life. I'm still not sure what really happened, but it totally changed my life.

Life continued. Dorsey and I became grandparents. There is no experience in life that quite measures up to the thrill of grandchildren. I have often quipped that grandchildren are God's reward for you not killing your kids in their teen years.

I continued substitute teaching and volunteering at WNOP. Life was full, my health had stabilized, and was beginning to have confidence that I could make an appointment and not end up in the hospital.

Early one morning, Dorsey came back to bed and said, "Bev, I don't understand this, but I feel that God told me our hard times are over, and that He will restore everything that has been lost in this illness.`" It was one of those times when, like Mary, I "kept all these things, and pondered them in [my] heart.`" (See Luke 2:19.)

In November we visited friends in Jackson, Tennessee. I was kneeling in prayer after the service when a woman stood beside me. She looked to be of medium height, slender, gray headed, and very regal. Dorsey remembers her as kind of dumpy, but her words will forever be imprinted on my brain.

She said, "I have been sent to tell you that the hard times are now over. God is going to restore everything that you have lost in this illness. From this point onward, you will make a slow but steady recovery."

Later we talked to Ron Brown, the pastor in Jackson, and I told him what the lady had said and how it was verbatim what Dorsey felt God had told him. The pastor asked what she looked like. I described her the best I could. He looked somewhat puzzled and said, "We don't have anyone like that here." Our friends, Stanley and Joan Holland, confirmed his statement.

I replied, "I don't know about that, but you had someone like that here this evening." An angel? I don't know, although it seems probable. What I do know is that her prophetic word has turned out to be true. I have not had a fast-paced recovery, but I am recovering and getting stronger by the day.

Chapter 9

Dorsey: More Challenges and Adjustments

The next seven years were . . . interesting. They were full of challenges and adjustments.

By mid-1993, Bev was on the mend from her heart surgery. Her nightly intravenous feedings supplied her nutrition, and she was beginning to gain a few pounds. After her heart surgery, she was hospitalized only three more times in 1993—once in September and twice in November. Her strength was improving. Life was looking better.

In late fall, Betty, a real estate agent in our church, suggested that we look for a house that we could buy based on my salary. Earlier in the year, prior to Bev's heart problems, we were choosing brick and carpet for the house we were going to have built. However, when the school district chose not to renew her contract for the coming school year because of her absenteeism, the contractor graciously allowed us to back out of the deal.

The decision to buy or build a house was a big step for us. We had rented a house since our return to St. Louis. I guess we thought subconsciously that our chances of returning to Germany were greater if home ownership did not encumber us. However, Betty's suggestion made sense. The timing seemed right.

Bev perused Betty's thick book of listings and marked the houses that interested her. She and Betty looked at thirty-two houses in one week. She finally walked into one home and said, "This is it!" The owner accepted our offer, and we celebrated the Christmas holidays in our new home.

Bev continued to have absorption problems. The doctors had originally said her remaining intestine would adjust to its reduced size, and her ability to absorb would return within six months. This would happen because the villi in the small bowel would elongate and therefore be able to absorb more nutrients. After six months had passed, the doctors said that within a year she would be fine. That was changed to "within two years." Finally, they quit talking about adaptation and concentrated on survival.

Much to our surprise, the Social Security Administration granted her application for disability on the first try. We had heard horror stories of long, bitter fights and were prepared for the inevitable. However, with the backing of her team of doctors and her medical history, we had no problems. Again, the Lord was gracious to us.

February 1994 found Bev back in the hospital, as did June, July—where she again celebrated her birthday—and

November. Sometimes bacteria were in the blood. Sometimes she was dehydrated. Sometimes the doctor needed to do more testing. Thankfully, she was at home for the Christmas holidays and the birth of our first granddaughter, Abigayle Leann Carlson, on December 27, 1994. (Grandparenthood was an easy adjustment!)

During many of Bev's hospital stays, she was able to witness to several nurses and patients as well as doctors. One time as she was being wheeled into her room, another patient recognized her. Kathy had been a friend at New Life Center but had moved away from the area and was no longer serving God. She sent word, asking Bev to visit her if she could. Bev could and did. And Kathy found her way back to God.

After additional health battles in February, March, and April 1995, Dr. Janet Todorzcuk, Bev's superb gastroenterologist, began talking about the need for a small bowel transplant. She said that Bev's "long-term survival" depended on it, for the continuing bouts of septicemia (bacteria in the blood) were taking their toll. That put things in perspective rather quickly.

Our health insurance company concurred with the doctor's assessment and arranged for us to go to the University of Wisconsin Hospital in Madison for a transplant evaluation in August 1995.

The reams of Bev's medical records formed almost a foot-high stack on the doctor's desk as he explained the operation. The hospital staff there had completed four intestinal transplants. Two were deemed successful. If Bev wanted one, she could have it. If her "long-term survival`" depended on the transplant, what choice did she have?

Twenty minutes later, we left for a tour of the hospital. She was placed on the organ transplant list and was given a beeper to carry. The beeper would signal when a donor had been found. She would *immediately* have to go to Madison, Wisconsin, for the surgery.

If she had the transplant, she would have to stay in Madison until the anti-rejection drugs could be regulated and she was stabilized. She would be on anti-rejection drugs for the rest of her life. All follow-up care would be at the university hospital. When she had bouts of rejection—not *if*, but *when*—she would immediately have to return to the hospital. They *strongly* suggested that we relocate to Madison to be near the hospital. That was what other families had done.

Relocating was not a viable option. Neither was I comfortable with everything having to be done in Madison. The distance was too far to drive when minutes counted. What if we couldn't get a flight out within the prescribed time limits? What if the rejection destroyed the donated intestine and another one was not available?

Bev carried the beeper for a year, but no donor became available. Because of Bev's size and because her abdominal cavity had shrunk, the doctors had told us the donor would have to be a child or a very small adult.

Finally, we petitioned our insurance company to allow the transplant to be done at Barnes-Jewish Hospital in St. Louis. The Barnes medical team had done an intestinal transplant on a ten-year-old boy. The surgery was successful. Even so, the child died only a month later due to other complications.

After the insurance company worked out the financial arrangements for the transplant with the hospital, Bev went through three days of evaluation and testing in August 1996. All their tests indicated that she still needed the transplant. However, before they listed her for an organ transplant, the medical team wanted to do one more test. (After all, Barnes-Jewish is a teaching hospital connected with the Washington University School of Medicine.) It was set for November, giving Bev time to recuperate after the General Conference of the United Pentecostal Church International in October in San Antonio.

Something happened, however, between August and November 1996. She checked into Barnes Hospital in early November for the final test. Her physical change between August and November so astounded the doctors that they put off the experiment. Instead of performing the intended procedure, they simply monitored her for a week. During that time interns paraded in and out of her room to listen to her rare heart murmur while Bev graciously introduced student nurses to the proper care of an ostomy.

At the end of the week the doctors concluded that her absorption rate had increased over *20 percent* in two to three months—a medical impossibility. They determined that she could now maintain her weight and health with what she could ingest and with shots to supply additional magnesium. The doctors stated that a small bowel transplant was not needed at this time or in the foreseeable future.

They could give no medical reason for the sudden change, but Bev could—and did! In December 1996, Bev's permanent IV line was removed.

Although Bev was hospitalized four more times in 1997, she lived without the nightly feedings. We enjoyed the freedom of not carting her pump and IV bags when we traveled.

Following Thanksgiving 1997, we drove to Jackson, Tennessee, to visit Stanley and Joan Holland, friends from Bible school days and former missionaries to Uruguay. Although we had planned to leave Sunday afternoon to return to St. Louis, we decided to attend the evening service with the Hollands at the Lighthouse United Pentecostal Church pastored by Ron Brown.

As Bev and I prayed between the pews that night, a lady in a purple suit tapped Bev on the shoulder and said she had a word from the Lord for her. Among other things, she said that beginning that night God was starting a slow but gradual healing process in her. From that point on, she would gradually get better.

That sounded good. We rejoiced in the encouraging words. Nevertheless, like Thomas, I wanted to see the improvement before I got too excited.

A week or two later, a bout with flu and other minor problems left Bev severely dehydrated. On December 11, Dr. Todorzcuk decided to hospitalize her for a "twenty-three-hour observation`" to rehydrate her. It seemed that

Murphy's law was in full force. Apparently, the devil was doing everything he could to cause us to doubt the words of the lady in purple.

While Bev was being rehydrated, Dr. Todorzcuk decided to insert a new IV line and start the nightly feedings on a temporary basis. Naturally, the surgical procedure and adjusting the TPN level extended her stay for another day or two. Then when Bev was dressing—expecting to be released in time to attend the World Network of Prayer volunteer luncheon at Margie Becton's home and the Foreign Missions Division's Christmas dinner later that evening—the doctor noticed that Bev's arm was swollen and discovered a blood clot. The clot had to be treated with blood thinners. Again, another disappointing delay.

A few days later, Bev got out of bed to go to the restroom. When she stood up, the IV line simply fell out of her arm! It had to replaced, but her blood was now *too thin* for surgery. She would have to have platelets to build up her blood. Another delay.

The "twenty-three-hour observation" ended December 24, just in time for the Christmas holidays. Nevertheless, the words of the lady in purple have proven true. Although there have been setbacks, Bev's health has continued to improve gradually. Now when she has a reaction to a pneumonia shot and her arm swells from her shoulder to her wrist (October 1999) or she becomes septic again (November 1999) or she has pancreatitis (January 2000), I cling to the promise of gradual healing.

In April 2000 Bev had surgery to remove her diseased gall bladder. (Long-term TPN can damage the gall bladder and liver.) The surgery was successful, but she developed a severe pain in her shoulder and her chronic knee pain persisted. The nurse told her that the air that was pumped into the abdominal cavity during the surgery probably settled in the shoulder area and was causing the pain.

CT scans were ordered for what we had expected to be her dismissal day. Afterward, an orthopedic doctor came in, looked at her, and declared that she had a torn rotator cuff and he was going to give her a cortisone shot. Bev reacts badly to all steroids; she becomes violent. It was quite evident that the doctor had not read her chart. She "politely`" informed him that he was not giving her cortisone. Miffed at her rebuff, he turned and left. She never had the shot. Her shoulder is fine. The nurse was apparently right.

Finally, the surgeon told Bev she could leave after an MRI, which was scheduled for 3:30 on Wednesday afternoon. She woke up from her nap in time for the test. She noticed that her right leg was hurting and thought she had somehow hurt it while she slept.

She was wheeled down to radiology for the MRI. However, because of her staples from the surgery, the test could not be given. So Bev got dressed and we packed her bags. The sky was dark as we hurried home, for the metropolitan area was in the throes of a tornado warning.

Bev's leg ached all night. On a scale of one to ten, she said it was ten-plus. She frequently cried out as cramps seized her leg and pain shot down through her calf.

The next morning, we heeded the doctor's advice and returned to the ER. Bev had the classic symptoms of a blood clot. Thankfully, the x-rays revealed a ruptured Baker's cyst but no clots. The doctor explained that the normal treatment for a ruptured Baker's cyst was to do nothing. He recommended Bev get a pair of crutches, stay off her feet for several days, and take pain pills.

Once again Bev lived up to her reputation. Who else would enter the hospital for gall bladder surgery and come home on crutches because of a ruptured Baker's cyst she did not know she had?

I marvel at God's irony and hope I am learning the lessons in patience He is trying to teach me. I'm beginning to think I have a spiritual learning disability in this area.

Chapter 10

Bev and Dorsey: Lessons from the Journey

After conducting a Faith Promise service in January 2000, Bev and I were talking to the pastor's wife and the assistant pastor as we sat around a table in the fellowship hall. Somehow Bev's illness became the topic of discussion. The assistant pastor asked, "Why do you think God allowed this to happen? What have you learned from it?"

Good questions! I don't know if anyone has ever been so sincere or straightforward with his questions.

The answer to the first question was fairly easy. God *allowed* the disease to come our way to help perfect us. Bev frequently states that God will be as gentle as He possibly can to accomplish His will. Some people hear His soft, still voice and obey. For others, such as Saul of Tarsus, it takes a more dramatic means of capturing one's attention. For us, it apparently took a debilitating illness for us to become pliable and submitted to His divine will and plan. He allowed it because He loves us too much to leave us as we were. *In His divine wisdom, He chose Crohn's disease because it was the best tool to mold and shape us to be more like Him.*

We must remember that fire refines gold. (See I Peter 1:7.) Years of extreme pressure deep within the earth and then the cutting, the grinding, and the polishing transform chunks of carbon into sparkling diamonds. The kneading and pressure of a potter's hand and then the fire of the kiln create graceful bowls from lumps of clay. Likewise, God uses persecution, financial difficulties, illness, and a wide array of other situations in life to help Christians mature and become more like Him.

As we mentioned earlier in this book, the J. B. Phillips translation of the Book of James states that we should welcome such situations into our lives and embrace them as dear friends because of the good they are doing in our lives. (We know that is easier said than done!)

Explaining what we have learned is much more involved. On a strictly human level, we learned that:

- Patients need to be proactive in their medical care. They should learn all they can about their disease and take some responsibility for their treatment. They should not passively sit back and allow the doctor to make all the decisions. The patients are uniquely created humans and will not always fit within the norms established in medical textbooks. They must tell the doctor what is going on and how their body is responding. If the doctor will not listen, they need to find one who will.
- Patients need to pay attention to what is happening around them. One of Bev's hospital stays was

extended because her blood pressure readings were around 175/125 while her normal readings are in the 90/60 range. After an additional CT scan, the doctor used a portable blood pressure monitor, and Bev's blood pressure dropped about fifty points. The blood pressure cuff at her bedside was faulty. Another time Bev stopped a nurse who had orders to give her a shot of a medicine to which she is allergic.

- Patients need to find a medical team that suits their personality. Some might need a quiet doctor while others need one with a more aggressive style. They should keep looking until they find one that they and their family are comfortable with. They should remember they are the consumers, while doctors are the providers. If they get a doctor who forgets his role, they can look him straight in the eye and say, "The last time I checked, *doctor* was not spelled *G-o-d*. This is still my body — which has not read your medical textbook — and I am still in charge." It is a doctor's duty to keep explaining until the patient is totally comfortable with his or her situation. The patient should settle for nothing less.

- Patients should learn the provisions of their health insurance policy. They should do everything they can to follow their policy's requirements about pre-authorizations and referrals. If a claim is denied, they should not be afraid to ask why and should check with their company's insurance clerk or call the carrier's customer service representative. If patients do not demand their rights, they can't expect anyone else to do it for them. They can do this and still be Christians — they just need to pray more during such times.

- No matter how terrible the situation may appear, someone is worse off. Patients should learn to count the blessings in life and see where they can help others.
- A strong support network is important when struggling with chronic illness. Don't try to do it by yourself. Allow others to help. Join support groups and learn from shared experiences.
- Chronic illness does not have to completely control one's life. The chronically ill person has a great need for normalcy. Life must continue, and he or she must be allowed to live life as normally as possible. This means that the caregiver needs to know when to step back to give the patient more freedom and when to set tighter boundaries. This has been one of my (Dorsey's) big frustrations. Bev puts her heart into everything she does, and sometimes I recognize when she has overextended herself before she does. It is difficult to know when to pull—and how hard to pull—the reins.
- Chronic illness affects more than just the patient. It impacts everyone closely associated with the patient. While those associated may not endure the physical pain, they suffer emotionally, mentally, and financially. When you pray for patients, remember their family members too.
- Chronic illness impacts each individual in his or her own unique way. Coping with Bev's illness made our daughter more mature and empathetic than others her age. Our son, however, had never known a healthy mother. He would retreat inside himself whenever she was hospitalized and would hide his feelings. In speaking of her hospital stay in February 2000, he said that was the first time he did not expect her to die.

Living with Crohn's disease has been a wonderful spiritual learning experience. (But one I would not choose for anyone else.) The lessons were difficult to learn and certainly not fun or entertaining. However, God knew what courses we needed. The major spiritual lessons we learned are:

- God is truly awesome. We could never begin to describe His holiness and majesty. His presence has been our shining light during the darkest nights. His love and kindness are beyond comprehension.
- God can be trusted. Twice in Matthew's Gospel, Jesus commanded His disciples to get in a boat and go to the other side of the Sea of Galilee. (See Matthew 8 and 14.) In each instance, a violent storm arose. The disciples found themselves in the storms *in the will of God*. However, it was not God's will for the storm to destroy them. It was His will for them to go to the other side. Yet in the storm, the disciples realized that He controlled the wind and waves and that He would not forsake them in times of trouble. Because of God's holiness and His love for us, He can be trusted. David said, "He leadeth me beside the still waters . . . though I walk through the valley of the shadow of death`" (Psalm 23:2, 4). We must get to the point in our Christian walk that our location is not the important thing. What is important is following the Leader. If we follow Him, He will always go before us and we will dwell in His presence. For those who struggle with trusting God, we highly recommend *Trusting God Even When Life Hurts* by Jerry Bridges, published by NavPress.

- Praise is one of the strongest weapons in the Christian's arsenal. More than lofty words and nice-sounding platitudes, praise is first a recognition of the might, majesty, and sovereignty of God. It is understanding His inherent holiness and purity, which keeps Him from anything vile or corrupt. It is knowing that His love for us far exceeds our comprehension and that, because of His love, He only wants what is best for us. As we praise Him, we release His power to do His creative work within us—even by using situations that we would normally avoid.
- Prayer is indispensable. A sign on a neighborhood church in Florissant, Missouri, stated, "Prayer is the oil for the daily grind." We must not only pray to survive the pressures of daily living, we must commune daily with God to keep our relationship with Him and to renew the power of the Holy Ghost within us. As personal relationships demand good communication, our relationship with God likewise demands we talk to Him long and often.
- We desperately need our brothers and sisters in Christ. Often in times of serious illness, we are too emotionally drained or too physically weak to pray for ourselves. That is when we must have the church to bear us up. The Gospels give us the example of the four friends who let a man down through the roof of a house so that Jesus could heal him.

While thinking about the past forty-plus years, I (Bev) realized something often overlooked. God can speak a body in or out of existence. This is not a great thing to Him.

But God cannot change an attitude or spirit. He can provide the climate, but the willingness to change has to be generated from a submissive and contrite Christian.

One night I became discouraged because of some problems with my colostomy. I asked God for a verse of Scripture, and Philippians 1:6 immediately came to mind: "Being confident of this very thing, that he which hath begun a good work in you will perform it until the day of Jesus Christ."

On four separate occasions, one of the goals of surgery has been to remove the rectal stump. Each time, for different reasons, it was not done. After the last surgery, the doctor admitted he was not sure why it was not done. But I do. The colostomy will be reversed. God has promised, and it will happen.

Crohn's disease has had a positive effect on me. I have learned how to praise. I have learned more about faith. In fact, I have developed my own definition of faith: *Faith is the ability to relax in adverse circumstances, knowing they are for our good.*

I do not know what the future holds, but with God's help, I will continue to raise my hands and sing, "I will praise Him . . . ."

Where will we go from here? I don't know, but I'm ready for a new adventure.

During my time with Crohn's disease, I began to look on life as a book with many chapters. Some chapters, the author may be thrilled to finish; others the author may be sad to add the final period. But there is always another chapter to begin.

Crohn's disease has not been easy to live with. I don't know anyone I dislike enough to wish it upon, but the process has been a growing and learning experience for me. I have learned to be thankful that God chose this disease to teach me some things He wanted me to learn.

Thanks to Crohn's disease I have learned to take time to enjoy life. I have learned the value of laughter; I have learned to appreciate my husband and children as well as my church family. I have learned that we can hold dreams only to see them slip through our hands. I know now that God is not a God who leaves holes in our lives. He will always provide something new to replace anything He has had to remove. I have learned that God will teach us lessons we have to know to get to Heaven, and He will do so as gently as possible. However, He is not above drastic measures if He has to use them.

An easier way to express my heart's feeling is, *I have learned.* I have been surprised at the value of these lessons. Often when I talk to people, they will say, "I couldn't tell just anybody this, but I know you will understand." God has used this disease for my good. What more can I say?

What will happen from here? I have no idea, but I'm eagerly looking forward to it.

Chapter 11

Dorsey: The Journey Continues

The chronology of our original book ended in 2000. Many things have transpired since then. For the most part, Bev's health has continued to improve, just as the lady in the purple suit prophesied. The problems with Crohn's disease seemed to be behind us and we were living with the effects of the disease.

Bev continued to take nightly IVs to supplement her fluid intake. Her IV lines continued to get infected and had to be replaced. (One lasted for almost seven years; others have lasted only a few weeks.) The infected lines usually led to sepsis (bacteria in the blood), which demanded another round of potent IV antibiotics. And the cycle continued.

We considered this our normal. We gladly lived with the inconvenience of making sure we carried IV bags, tubing, and ostomy supplies—and always stayed alert for the next restroom—whenever we traveled at home or abroad. Thankfully, Bev's health had improved to the point that we were willing to consider overseas travel.

Consequently, the Lord has allowed us to be involved in several different mission fields.

As an associate minister with Global Missions, I have a travel account for our travel expenses outside of North America. (If you would like to contribute, contact Global Missions.) To us, taking our allotted vacation time to minister overseas was a no-brainer.

After being tethered to North America for twenty years, our first overseas trip was in 2001. I was a part of the Follow the Fire Crusade team for Lagos, Nigeria, along with Steve Spears, Scott Loyd, and Doug Klinedienst. It was an eye-opening experience that gave me a much greater appreciation for the missionaries in Africa and a thankfulness that we had been called to Europe. However, seeing two thousand people receive the Holy Ghost in one night was well worth trip.

I flew from Lagos to Munich, Germany, where Bev met me at the airport. (By the way, the airlines do not expect four one-cubic-foot boxes when they say you can carry your medicine on board.) We then attended the Follow the Fire Crusade in Augsburg. It was so refreshing to be back in Germany and to watch God's Spirit being poured out in the crusade.

The resident missionary left Augsburg in 2002 and put a young man in charge of the church. Missionary Charles Stovall was still deputizing and wouldn't be able to return to the field for a few more months. He asked if I would be willing to go over to Augsburg for a few weeks to keep an eye on things. Would I be willing! Thankfully, I still had two weeks of vacation and the division granted me a leave of absence for two extra weeks.

That resulted in me spending the month of December based in Augsburg. Bev joined me in the middle of the month. It was delightful to meet Horst and Sharon Krauss, the young pastor and his wife, in Augsburg. His leadership ability was readily evident, and I knew the former missionary had made a wise choice. I kept busy preaching, teaching in the Bible school, and doing prayer drives in the area.

The highlight of the month was going to Budapest, Hungary, to celebrate Christmas with the missionaries appointed to Eastern Europe: Sam and Pat Balca, our hosts; Mike and Jill Patterson, Romania; Roger and Becky Buckland, Czech Republic; Harold and Helen Kinney, Austria. It was our first time in Eastern Europe, and I was shocked at how modern the cities were.

At the end of 2003, Bev and I flew to Malta for special New Year's services with missionaries Kirby and Mary Parker. Malta was a new field, and we were excited to be involved in a new work. Two things that impressed me were the many people who knew Kirby Parker by name and the horrible conditions of Malta's narrow roads.

In 2004 I flew to Okinawa for Pentecost Sunday services with the GIs in the Asian Military Ministry with missionaries Rufus and Pam Parker. The Parkers were extraordinary hosts and sent me the schedule for the week,

Ray and Judi Nicholls stand with Bev before the cathedral in Kraków, Poland.

detailing planned activities, suggested attire, and weather forecasts. I was impressed! I also was thrilled to see God move in the services and the hunger for God by those who defend our nation. It also was good to see missionaries David Doan and Ed Hosmer, who visited the services.

Later that year Bev and I flew to Warsaw, Poland, to be with Ray and Judi Nicholls. Construction and roadwork were everywhere as the nation strived to modernize to meet membership requirements for the EU. What a privilege it was to travel to several different cities and see the work the Nichollses were establishing!

I jokingly told Ray that one highlight of the trip was changing his flat, steel-belt-exposed tire in the rain. I was thankful that God had protected us on the wet, winding, hilly roads and had provided a level area for the tire exchange. I also encouraged him to requisition new tires for his Sheaves for Christ auto. He was just being a good missionary and trying to stretch the donors' dollars.

From Warsaw, we flew to the Czech Republic to teach in the Bible school in Prague. Roger and Becky Buckland were establishing a work in one of the most beautiful cities in Europe. Their church building was what had once been the private chapel for a nobleman and his family. It was a unique setting in which to see the Spirit of God do His work.

Bev and I returned to Malta in the spring of 2005. Danny and Jeanne Beth Hance, a member of Global Missions, accompanied us. Danny promoted home Bible studies, Jeanne Beth sang, and Bev and I ministered the Word. It was so wonderful to see the growth in the Maltese church.

In 2006 Gary and Linda Reed invited us to teach a leadership seminar in Jordan at the Dead Sea. It was our first time to be in a predominantly Muslim country. Of course, the weekend was busy with different services in the greater Amman area.

The leaders of the Jordanian church, including missionaries Gary and Linda Reed (back row) and the late Cindy White (kneeling).

An added blessing to our trip was traveling with the Reeds to ancient Petra and then on to Israel, as Sister Reed had a doctor's appointment in the northern part of the nation. In four days, the Reeds did their best to show us the Dead Sea, Jerusalem, Bethlehem, Caesarea, and the Sea of Galilee. We arrived back to their house in time to repack and then hurry to the airport for our early morning flight to St. Louis.

Chapter 12

For Bev: International Traveler

With my health fairly stable, Dorsey and I began to think of overseas travel. He was asked to be a part of the Follow the Fire crusade in Lagos, Nigeria. We decided I would meet at the airport in Munich after the crusade in Nigeria and then attend the Follow the Fire Crusade in Augsburg, Germany.

Flying to Munich was my first overseas trip by myself since coming home from Europe in 1981. I would would have to negotiate the travel pitfalls by myself.

I called the airlines, and they confirmed that I could carry my medication on board. However, the infusion company had packed my twelve IV bags in four one-cubic-foot boxes, which were insulated with Styrofoam. The porter helped me get my luggage and boxes to the check-in counter. The attendant did a double take when I said the boxes were my medication that I was told I could carry on.

There are times to be independent and self-sufficient. And there are times to be needy. This was one of those times. I explained that my life depended on receiving IV fluids at night, otherwise I would dehydrate. Eventually a compromise was worked out. The boxes would go as checked luggage, but I would not be charged since they contained medication.

The next hurdle was clearing customs in Munich. Dorsey had ordered a wheelchair for me when he purchased the tickets. The porter gathered my boxes and luggage on a trolley and pushed me and the trolley to the front of the VIP line. In no time, the immigration officers stamped my passport, the porter wheeled me through the exit, and Dorsey embraced me.

It felt so good to be back in Germany. Bobby and Tanya Lewis were the resident missionaries in Augsburg. Tom Johnson and Paul Elder were the crusade speakers. The Spirit of God moved, and the altars filled with people seeking God.

My German was pretty rusty, so I lingered back from the altar and prayed. As I prayed, I saw a gigantic urn above the altar that was tipped so a single drop was about to spill out. The Lord spoke to me and said the urn contained the prayers we had prayed for Germany and although we were no longer appointed missionaries to Germany, He wanted me to see the revival that was about to be poured out. My heart was so full I thought it would burst.

I survived with flying colors my first overseas trip since being forced to come home in 1981 because of my illness. I felt liberated and couldn't wait until we could go again.

The only hassles I had with traveling were making sure my medical supplies were packed properly and I passed through TSA or other foreign security measures. On overseas flights, I always carried one IV bag on board so I could hook up during the flight and maintain my hydration. Sometimes that presented problems.

One time I was patted down by an agent who felt my IV lines. She immediately said she could not let me board. Even after showing her documentation from my doctor, she still refused to allow me to walk down to the gate. Finally, she called her supervisor who explained the way more fully to her.

I solved my boarding problems in St Louis by contacting TSA and explaining my health situation and the need for the supplemental hydration. The local officers were wonderful and worked out a system for me. I would notify them in advance of our pending flights. When I arrived at the airport, TSA would send a supervisor down to meet me and to walk us through security. Usually this resulted in a private screening. A couple of times I had an agent whose sister had Crohn's and fully understood my problems. She was so helpful.

I loved every place we went! Each country offers new opportunities and challenges.

Let me tell you about our first trip to Poland with Ray and Judi Nicholls. They are simply some of the best missionaries we have. They had a headquarters church in

Warsaw and several works scattered across Poland. We visited four or five of these works in places I can't even pronounce. This gave us a great opportunity to see the countryside. Dorsey preached, and I testified.

The Nichollses took us sightseeing at Krakow. It's a beautiful city dominated by the cathedral. We shopped in the market and visited with some vendors. Then we decided to go to the cathedral and see the sarcophagi of the Polish kings. We started to enter the crypt, but the guard indicated the entrance was farther down on the right. Dorsey went through the next doorway and we followed. There were steps going up. That seemed strange, but it seemed to be the way the man had directed us.

It wasn't too long before we realized we were on the stairs leading to the bell tower. With people behind us, we had no choice but to keep going up.

Judi and Dorsey hate heights. They both stood at the rear of the tower while Ray and I snapped pictures from the open window. Ray cautioned Judi not to lean against the wall as it might crumble.

Finally, we had enough fun at their expense and started down. The stairs seemed much steeper going down than they had going up. Dorsey led the way. He leaned back and rested his arms on the railing, thinking he could catch himself if he lost his footing. Ray was at the back, making comments about the building shaking that put Judi in tears.

All at once I was struck by how funny we must look to God. Dorsey was crab-walking down the stairs. I was laughing hysterically. Judi was crying. And Ray continued his dry humor about the danger of the tower collapsing.

Another memorable trip was going to Jordan to speak at the leadership seminar for national leaders and to preach on the weekends. As a "reward" for our "sacrifice," Gary and Linda Reed took us on a four-day whirlwind trip of Petra and Israel. Naturally we could not stay long in any one spot.

The first day we left Amman, Jordan's capital, around eight o'clock in the morning and drove several hours to Petra. Nothing can really prepare you for the first glimpse of the carved building in Petra as you turn the corner in the Siq. It is simply breathtaking!

After a couple of hours in Petra, we drove on to Eilat on the Red Sea and spent the night. The second morning we cleared Israeli immigration and drove along the Dead Sea to Jerusalem. After dinner, we went to Bethlehem and stayed at the hotel owned by Brother Tinnas's family.

On the third day, we visited the market in Old Town Jerusalem and then went to the Mount of Olives and the Wailing Wall. The weather was very windy, and at one point it literally lifted me off the ground. I joked that I wasn't the only one translated from the Mount of Olives. From there we traveled north to Caesarea, stopping long enough to see the Roman ruins in the dark before going to our hostel.

The fourth day, Linda Reed had a doctor's appointment. Afterward we drove to the Sea of Galilee, then hurried back to Amman after lunch. We arrived in time for us to repack our suitcases and head to the airport.

Security was tight at the airport for our late-night flight. I traumatized the security agent. She had never dealt with anyone who had an ostomy bag.

Chapter 13

Dorsey: Life, Death, and Social Security

Allow me to interrupt the travelog to tell of another miracle. As previously stated, when Bev's short-gut problem became apparent in 1992, the doctors filled out the paperwork so she could receive disability benefits from Social Security. As her health improved, she began to substitute teach. From the start, she kept meticulous records and reported her earnings to the local SS office because of the earning cap. Finally, they told her to quit bothering them as it was confusing, and they would monitor her earnings.

Eventually she started working full time as the receptionist/secretary in Global Missions. Every year she would get a statement from Social Security stating that her earning for 19xx was $xxxx and her new benefit for the coming year would be so much. She questioned if she should still be eligible for the benefits as she was working full time, but it was evident that Social Security was monitoring her earnings and kept sending her checks.

Imagine our surprise and distress when we received a letter demanding we repay $26,704 within thirty days to Social Security for overpayment of disability benefits! Naturally, we appealed and sent a thick stack of documents to them for review.

Finally, we had a date to meet the judge. His demeanor was menacing. His first sneery comment was, "Do you *really* think you deserve these benefits?" Again we explained how Bev had tried to report the earnings and was told to quit as Social Security would monitor her wages.

The night before we met the judge, I felt led to go down to my office and look for anything else that might support our case. I found a letter stating that she had earned $xxxx in 19xx and her new benefit for the following year would be so much. When I showed that to the judge, his demeanor seemed to soften. He told us he would review the case and get back with us.

Somewhere along this process in 2007, Bev developed a fungal growth on a heart valve. It was a life-and-death situation as it was much more serious than the bacterial infections she had had before. Thanks to prayers and medical expertise, she gradually began to recover, and the doctor began discussing follow-up care.

I was scheduled to fly to Myanmar to teach Romans to the Bible school students a few days after she was to be released. The doctor saw no reason for me not to go and Bev encouraged me to go. So I went reluctantly, unaware of the side effects of the drug.

The follow-up care for the fungal growth was daily infusions with amphotericin B at the hospital's infusion center. We were later told that the nurses call the drug "ampho-terrible." I later read on the Internet:

> Amphotericin B is well known for its severe and potentially lethal side effects. Very often, it causes a serious reaction soon after infusion (within 1 to 3 hours), consisting of high fever, shaking chills, hypotension, anorexia, nausea, vomiting, headache, dyspnea and tachypnea, drowsiness, and generalized weakness. The violent chills and fevers have been nicknamed "shake and bake." ("Shake and Bake." TheFreeDictionary.com. Retrieved 2016-12-09; Hartsel, Scott. *Studies on Amphotericin B.* (PDF). *Archived* (PDF) from the original on 20 December 2016. *Retrieved 8 December 2016.* As quoted in ttps://en.wikiped-ia.org/wiki/Amphotericin_B#-Side_effects Accessed August 18, 2018.)

Bev said if she were faced with the same decision again, she would probably choose not to take the medicine as the side effects were horrible.

Missionaries Ray and Judi Nicholls were deputizing during this time. Judi checked in on Bev and realized she needed help. I will be forever grateful that Judi stayed with Bev during the duration of the infusions.

Both Ray and Judi were with Bev when the letter came from the Social Security judge. Fearful, Bev asked Ray to open and read the letter. The judge's decision was "fully favorable"! He concurred that Social Security had been monitoring Bev's wages and should have curtailed the disability benefits. But since they did not, we were not at fault! God erased the almost $27,000 debt that we could not have repaid!

Bev called me while I was in Yangon and told me the news. What a heavy load was lifted! I felt terrible about leaving Bev, especially when I learned of her struggles with the drug. However, I was glad I had put His kingdom first, and He had honored the sacrifice by sending Judi Nicholls and by deleting the debt!

Dorsey teaching Romans at the Bible school in Yangon, Myanmar (Burma). Superintendent J.Ral Buai was interpreting.

Chapter 14

For Bev: Miracles

The demand for repayment of the disability money from Social Security was frightening. I had done everything I knew to do to be honest and above board, reporting my earnings to them weekly. Finally, they said I was confusing them and to stop the reporting. They said they would monitor my earnings.

A friend had told me that once you receive disability, it is difficult to get off the rolls. I realized I was earning more than the limits allowed for a disabled worker. I wondered when it would stop. In 2003, we received a letter stating SSA would be reevaluating my disability claim. We were planning to remodel our main bathroom, but postponed construction until the matter was resolved. When the checks kept coming, we went ahead with the remodel and were pleased with the outcome.

Naturally, we appealed the repayment of nearly $27,000. When we finally met with the SSA judge, it was apparent that he had already decided against us. Dorsey had sent him a thick file of documents supporting our contention that SSA was monitoring my wages and any overpayment was their fault.

The night before our meeting, Dorsey felt led to make one more search of his office to see if he could find more documentation. He found a letter from SSA stating that my earnings for the year xxxx was $xxxx and my monthly benefit for the coming year would be $yyyy.

When the judge sarcastically asked if we really thought I deserved the disability payment, we replied we questioned why I was still receiving them. Then Dorsey showed him the letter he had found, proving that SSA was indeed monitoring my wages.

The judge's demeanor changed as he looked at the letter. He put it with the file with the other documentation and said he would look it over and then inform us of his findings.

I don't know if the stress from the Social Security mess weakened my already reduced immune system, but I developed a fungal infection on my heart valve. The infection looked like a lump with a casing on the valve. I knew this was more serious than my other bouts of sepsis. The infectious disease doctor gave me super strong antifungal medications. By the grace of God, I survived. Years later my cardiologist would say that as far as he knew, I was the only patient who had survived a fungal infection on the heart valve.

I was improving, and the doctor was preparing for follow-up care. Dorsey was scheduled to fly to Thailand and then on to Myanmar with missionary Robert Frizzell. He had been asked to teach the Book of Romans. Dorsey asked the doctor if he should cancel his trip. The doctor did not see any reason to do so, so I encouraged him to go ahead.

The follow-up care consisted of a daily round of a drug called amphotericin, which had to be administered at the hospital's infusion center. It turned out to be one of the worse experiences of my life. The drug is called "Shake and Bake`" by many in the medical community. Within three hours after the infusion, I would run a high fever and then have extreme chills that caused me to shake uncontrollably. This was accompanied by headaches and nausea. It was all I could do to drive myself to and from the infusion center.

Ray and Judi Nicholls are missionaries to Poland, Belarus, and Ukraine. They also are wonderful friends. They were on deputation, and Judi called to see how I was doing. When she learned of the "shake and bake," she immediately decided she would come and care for me. I will always be grateful for her love and concern. How providential it was for her to be on deputation and free to help me!

If I were given the choice whether to have amphotericin again or die, I think I would choose to be with Jesus. The amphotericin is much like having chemotherapy without hair loss.

Ray had a few days without deputation services, so he came to be with his wife. He was there when the letter came from Social Security. I was no shape physically or emotionally to open the letter, so I asked Ray to read it.

Reluctantly, he tore open the envelope and read the letter. I carefully watched his face for any reaction. His crooked smile gave me hope. And then he read the letter aloud. The judge had decided in our favor. We did not have to repay the $26,704.

I called Dorsey in Myanmar and rejoiced with him over the phone. It was another miracle. Thank you, Jesus!

Chapter 15

Dorsey: More Fields

Bev's health continued about the same with nightly IVs and the occasional hospitalization. We were living our "normal."

In October 2007, Bev and I flew to Thessaloniki, Greece, to preach the Greek national conference. It was a delight to be with Sim and Judy Strickland, who are some of our personal Partners in Missions. I was honored to meet several Greek national leaders. Walking the streets of ancient Philippi with Sim Strickland helped to make the New Testament come alive to us.

We stayed closer to home in 2008 and went to Belize in Central America for the national conference. The conference was in the Mayan area of southern Belize. As her parents, Jerry and Brenda Sawyer, were on furlough, missionary Amy Sawyer led the services and translated for me. Having a woman in any type of leadership conflicts with Mayan culture. In spite of the tension and seeming lack of response, thirty-one people said they had received the Holy Ghost for the first time.

At the close of the conference, several Mayan couples came forward to be married. The brides were in white wedding gowns of various styles, and the grooms wore ties. Those who already had children had them to stand beside them.

Bev and Karen, Amy Sawyer's secretary, climbed to the top of one of the Mayan temples.

Amy Sawyer was a great hostess and took us to see the Mayan ruins. Bev and Karen, Sister Sawyer's secretary, climbed to the top of one of the temples.

In 2009 I accepted missionary Robert Frizzell's challenge to teach Epistles to pastors at a seminar in Phnom Penh, Cambodia. With the limited time, I knew it had to be a survey course. But being as concise and focused as I was, it was too much material. At their request, I sent Brother Frizzell my notes, which he had translated and distributed to the pastors.

Three things stand out to me about Cambodia: (1) The pastors' hunger for the Word of God. (2) The thirty-some people who were baptized in the Mekong River. (3) The absolute horror of the killing fields where collectively more than a million people were killed and buried by the Khmer Rouge.

In 2010, missionaries J. Prince and Suzana Mathiasz and the congregation at the beautiful Mt. Lavina headquarters church lavishly welcomed us to the picturesque island of Sri Lanka for Easter services.

Brother Mathiasz has given visionary leadership to the Sri Lanka church. One example is the national campground, on which he has planted sandalwood and mahogany trees as well as pineapple and other crops. The trees will provide long-term, future income for the church, while the pineapple and other crops will meet the more immediate needs. (Bev and I actually planted some of the trees and seedlings!)

The Mathiaszes took us to several country churches and showed us the beauty of their land. In one church I had to use two interpreters, both Sinhalese and Tamil, which I found challenging. A highlight of the trip for Bev was washing an elephant at a river near the elephant orphanage.

In 2012, we accepted Bill Markham's invitation to minister in Portugal and Spain. His unexpected death on October 21, 2016, makes our memories of being with him more precious. Knowing the challenges he faced with an invalid wife in California made his accomplishments on the field seem that much greater. Bill was a great friend, whose sacrifice I honor.

Chapter 16

For Bev: Retreats

Back in the '90s, former missionaries Robert Johnson, H. E. Gerald, and John Brian recognized the need to help veteran missionaries transition back to North America, and thus helped to establish the Veterans of Global Missions Association. Dorsey was elected the VGMA secretary in 2009. That meant that I also became more involved in the group.

The main purpose of the VGMA is to welcome former missionaries back home and assist them in settling into their role of pastor or retired missionary. Sometimes, the culture shock of returning to North America is as great or greater than when the missionaries go to their fields.

The two main events of the association are the annual banquet/business meeting at General Conference and the biennial veteran missionary retreat. The VGMA vice chairman's responsibility is planning the banquet. However, all VGMA executives and wives get involved in planning the retreats. That's the part I really enjoyed.

The first couple of retreats were held at Innsbrook, Missouri. Then we went to the YMCA of the Ozarks in Potosi, Missouri. The YMCA offered a lot of activities for the veterans such as fishing, archery, shooting, and hiking. It also offered a great venue for devotions and playing group games.

The last two VGMA retreats have been at the Lodge at Pere Marquette State Park, just north of Grafton, Illinois. It also offers fishing and hiking and the surrounding area tempts with ziplines—which I would really like to do—antiquing, and shopping. However, for the most part, the veteran missionaries simply enjoy fellowshipping with each other and sharing stories.

In April 2010, Dorsey and I were having lunch with Don and Saundra Hanscom—he was the VGMA chairman—at Red Robin in St. Peters, Missouri. We had just picked up supplies at Sam's for the gift bags for the retreat at the YMCA and were eating before making the hour or so drive. As we were waiting for our meals, I felt an itching sensation on my hip. I excused myself and went to the restroom to see what was going on. I discovered I had a blister-like rash of some kind.

After we arrived, I went online to see if I could determine what the rash was. It looked like shingles. The next day I visited the doctor in Potosi. He confirmed my Internet diagnosis and prescribed medication. The doctor had practiced as a medical missionary in Kenya and was well acquainted with Crohn's. He seemed divinely picked to treat me.

The medication helped the shingles to dry up. However, the pain has never left. At times the neuropathy is almost unbearable. Thankfully, it is somewhat tolerable with lidocaine patches in the day and Lyrica at night.

The shingles pain has not kept me from traveling. I have enjoyed every field that we have visited. I guess it isn't too surprising that Eastern Europe has stolen my heart.

In 2014 we flew to Budapest and met missionaries Steve and Jean Tir. The two cities of Buda and Pest merged in 1873. Buda, with the royal castle, is on the west side of the Danube River, while Pest is on the east. Together they form a gorgeous city. I would like to go back someday to visit the museums.

We met the Tirs in Budapest and from there we drove through Hungary and on to Serbia, a former part of Yugoslavia. Dorsey was tasked with teaching Church History to the combined student body of the two Bible colleges, while I got to have a session with the ladies.

We were so honored to be with Brother and Sister Jeroslav Andrasik and Brother and Sister Martin Sirka. Sister Sirka made the most delicious cabbage rolls for us.

The older ladies with their headscarves fascinated me. Having lived through the communist persecution of the church, they undoubtedly had stories to tell. I wish I had had time simply to listen to them testify and tell of God's goodness.

Perhaps my favorite trip was to Kiev, Ukraine, with Ray and Judi Nicholls. Ray Nicholls is the area coordinator for the nations that comprised the old USSR. The saints there immediately stole my heart. Their worship was so deep and moving. If I have the story correct, the pastor's grandfather was martyred by the communists for preaching the gospel. Later, the family immigrated to the US and did well. However, Pastor Sergey Tomev felt called to return to his homeland. Some of his siblings have joined him.

One of the young men in the church in Kiev is rated as the number-one cellist in Ukraine. He travels internationally to play his cello. He also plays in church. Hearing him play is enrapturing.

If I were younger and healthier, I would want to receive a missionary appointment to Ukraine.

Chapter 17

Dorsey: Heart Surgery #2

When Bev had her first open-heart surgery in 1993, the doctor told us she would need her heart valve replaced within five years. Our cardiologist monitored her valve with every visit and frequently reminded us that the valve would need to be replaced—"sometime in the near future." That near future became reality in 2013—twenty years after the doctor first told us it needed to be replaced.

Surgery was scheduled for mid-October, 2013, with a world renowned thoracic and cardiac surgeon. Dr. Nordlicht knew surgery was necessary but feared Bev would not survive. On the other hand, the surgeon was confident in his abilities and paid no heed to Nordlicht's concerns.

As the hours passed, I grew more worried. I was so thankful for the waiting room full of friends, family, and fellow ministers. Finally, the surgeon came out and said everything was fine and he would be back out in about an hour after everything was done. We waited. However, he never came back to speak to us.

Waiting room support group: L-R, Garry Tracy, Jim Poitras, Mike and Mariam Sponsler, Steve Judd, Krystin Carlson, Christina Burk, Darline Royer, Linda Poitras, John and Shirley Leaman, Sharon and Richard Davis. Some had left; others would come. There's nothing like family and the family of God during a crisis.

Finally, the elevator doors opened, and the nurses wheeled Bev into the ICU. She was alive but in the la-la-land of post-surgery. She kept requesting something to drink, but she was restricted to sponges to moisten her mouth.

During the night she wanted to ask again for something to drink. In her drug-induced daze, she reached around to grab the call button and yanked on the cord. However, instead of the call button, she jerked out the IV line imbedded in her chest, causing blood to spurt all over. You can imagine the chaos.

When I arrived early the next morning, telltale signs of the emergency still existed. The staff was preparing to wheel Bev down to Interventional Radiology for them to insert a new catheter.

On the follow-up visit, Dr. Nordlicht called the surgeon by name and said, "He really earned his money this time."

First, the surgeon had difficulty getting the lung-heart bypass machine in place because of Bev's small chest cavity. Second, he was surprised that the right atrium wall was so thin due to the earlier surgery to excise the bacteria. He expressed concern that the wall might not be strong enough to carry the spark to restart the heart.

There's more to this story, but Bev needs to tell it.

About a month after Bev's heart surgery, I had both knees replaced. By having both done at the same time, I did not favor one knee over the other, and recovery time was cut in half. I went directly from the hospital to a rehab center and had three hours of therapy a day. My physical therapist was fantastic and had me walking up and down steps before I went home ten or eleven days later.

In 2014 Bev and I went to Serbia with missionaries Steven and Jean Tir to teach in Bible school and preach weekend services. Knowing the persecution that the saints had endured under communism, it was so thrilling to see such a vibrant church. The thirst for knowledge by the Bible school students and the quality of leadership gave me great hope for the church.

The following year, Ray Nicholls arranged for Bev and me to teach faculty development classes in Kiev, Ukraine. Pastor Sergey Tomev and saints were incredible! The music and worship were heavenly! The nation's leading cellist plays during the worship service.

Back row: Members of the faculty for the Greek Bible school
Front row: Bev and Dorsey Burk, Sim and Judy Strickland

In April 2016 Bev and I returned to Greece to teach GATS faculty development classes for the Bible school. The quality and education of the faculty surpassed my expectations. It was our first time to be in Athens and we were thrilled to see the vitality of the congregation of diverse nationalities.

Chapter 18

For Bev: Heart Surgery Again

In 1993, the heart surgeon had said that within five years I would need a new heart valve. That became a reality twenty years later in October 2013. Doctor Nordlicht was fearful about the outcome, but knew it needed to be done. I called Krystin and explained the surgery and downplayed the fears. My daughter-in-law Christina, Dr. Nordlicht's assistant at that time, was fully aware, and I hoped the two girls wouldn't talk.

Dr. Nordlicht chose the leading heart surgeon in the Barnes/Washington University community to operate. This world-renowned surgeon travels internationally to teach and to operate. Confident of his abilities, he cast aside Dr. Nordlicht's fears.

Of course, I was apprehensive. But I was tired of having no energy and difficulty in breathing if I over exerted myself. I was ready for that to be over—however the Lord chose to do it.

As I was prepped for surgery in October, the nursing team was amazed at the number of people waiting for me. Krystin told me later that they prayed and watched the Cardinals game.

During the surgery, I had two or three out-of-body experiences. It may have been one with different scenes.

The first time I was floating above the operating table. I could see the doctors and nurses frantically working on me. I couldn't tell what was wrong, but I knew they were having problems.

Later I was in a bridge-like corridor that connects two buildings at Barnes-Jewish Hospital. I could see Christina desperately trying to reach someone on her telephone. The surgeon had not returned to talk to the family, and she knew something was wrong. She was hoping to find out what it was.

As I looked down on her, the Lord asked if I wanted to go Home or stay down here. I had thought about this several times before. I knew Dorsey could survive by himself and that he had the support of the church and Global Missions. Krystin had Kent and the girls. Devon had Christina and the kids. But Christina didn't seem to have anyone to encourage her and help her grow in Christ. So, because of Christina, I chose to stay on earth.

Shortly after that I saw myself reentering my body on the operating table. I knew I would live.

Later Christina and I were talking about the surgery and how scared they all were because the surgeon never came back to talk to them. She said she had gone to the bridge to call Dr. Nordlicht to see if he or his office staff had heard anything. She said, "And, Mom, you were there. I felt you right behind me. I know you were there." And then I told her about seeing her and choosing to stay behind to help her. We both cried.

It took several months to regain my strength and to really become active again. This wasn't easy for me. After all, the problem had been fixed and I was ready to move on. I soon discovered that the heart heals on its and on God's timeline and not Bev's.

As I became stronger, Dorsey and I were finally able to go back to our first love, missions. We went back to Poland in 2015 to be with the Nicholls and to go to Kiev, Ukraine, to teach faculty education courses and to preach on Sunday. I absolutely fell in love with the saints there. It was hard to put into words as I tried to share this new love with Krystin. I just babbled. The worship was heavenly even though it was in Ukrainian. The Spirit of God moved in an overwhelming way.

I was enraptured by the cellist. Brother Vlad is rated the number-one cellist in the nation. At Brother Nicholls's request, he played a solo of the song "Still I Will Trust Him." It was absolutely beautiful! Unfortunately, we had to leave for the airport before the altar service was over. I left Ukraine changed. I knew my decision to stay was the right one. Despite some worries I still had in the back of my mind, I once again made the choice to praise and still trust Him. I felt that song was just for me.

In 2016 Sim and Judi Strickland invited us back to Greece to teach faculty education courses. As long as my health held out, there was no way I was missing Greece! I missed teaching. It was a passion that never left me.

Later, Dorsey showed Krystin the pictures of me teaching in Greece. I was using my hands and whole body. Krystin just laughed and laughed. Despite just having heart surgery and as a fifth-generation educator, I guess teaching with everything I had was in my genes.

It's always enjoyable to be with the Stricklands. The Bible school is in Athens, and one of the men in the church was assigned to be our guide. He took us to the Acropolis. I overheard Dorsey tell him that we would stay at the base of the hill as he didn't think I could make the arduous climb up to the Parthenon. I rested a couple of times along the way, but I made it! I was proud of myself, and I knew Dorsey was too.

As a thank you gift for ministering, the Athens church gave me an oil painting of the Parthenon, which hangs in our living room. It reminds me of my many physical miracles and how God never took teaching away from me, despite not having a classroom anymore.

Another highlight of 2016 was my retirement! Truthfully, there were many times that I never thought I'd reach retirement. Yet, with God's grace, I retired from Global Missions just before General Conference in Indianapolis. In fact, Dorsey drove to the hotel and then I switched to the driver's seat and drove on to South Bend to see Krystin and her family.

I knew I really needed to retire. I was constantly tired and often had to force myself to keep going. Mary Schroeder had been a long-time employee at Global Missions. In fact, she was hired in February 1975 to be Dorsey's secretary. She retired a few years ago with great plans to travel and enjoy her hobbies. However, she died of cancer within a year or so of her retirement. I did not want that. I wanted to have time to enjoy my family, to continue our overseas ministry, and live a full life. I didn't want my family to miss out on things because I refused to stop when I knew I needed to. Retirement was bittersweet. I didn't want to be bored at home and I really didn't want to leave missions. Yet, retirement was right for me.

One of the things I had been saying for years was that I missed the Boston Terrier we had when the kids were younger. I had repeatedly told my family I wanted one when I retired. Much to my surprise, the missionaries at the 2016 School of Missions presented me with money to buy one upon my retirement. I was like a new mother, sending pictures to my kids and grandkids. As soon as he was old enough, Janko (Serbian for "John" or "Gift of God") came to live with a retired grandma.

Apparently, being retired was too boring for me as I started to have trouble breathing. I thought it was my heart and tried to slow down but things weren't improving.

Dorsey later told me that he had to call 911. The fact I didn't argue, or even question, let him know how sick I really was. Much of what happened during that hospitalization is fuzzy. I only have snippets of memory. I remember feeling like I was suffocating. I remember Krystin singing "Breath of God, Breathe on Me." I remember Christina being with me at all hours. I remember being told that both girls were bullying the doctors into taking better care of me. Later, the girls told me that Christina would tell Krys what was needed and Krystin would use her "principal" voice to get it done.

I woke up in Barnes-Jewish Hospital, healed once again.

Chapter 19

Dorsey: 2016-2017

Miraculously, Bev retired from Global Missions in September 2016. I say miraculously because we never expected her to live long enough to retire. I informed Bruce Howell, the director of Global Missions, and my boss Jim Poitras, the director of Education and Short-term Missions, of my decision to retire January 6, 2017. My hire anniversary was January 4, so by continuing until January 6, I would complete the first week of the new year and end thirty-eight years and two days in the Global Missions office. If our service in Jamaica and Germany are factored in, we have forty-three years of missionary service.

As my retirement approached, I focused on completing several textbooks for the Global Association of Theological Studies (GATS). Even though plans called for me to continue editing and designing the GATS books in my retirement, I wanted the current projects finished.

In mid-December 2016, Bev woke up, unable to breathe. I called 911, and the ambulance took her to the nearest hospital. She was admitted to the acute care unit because of pulmonary problems.

When my daughter-in-law Christina, who by this time was an oncology nurse at Barnes-Jewish, came to see Bev, she "explained the way more perfectly" to the nurses. Bev had not received her normal medications. She was not on an IV drip, which was customary in the hospital because of Bev's problems with dehydration and renal disease. The real fault was in the doctors' failure to read the medical history and write proper orders for the nurses.

From that point on, we tried to get her moved to Barnes-Jewish Hospital where most of her regular doctors practiced. However, we were told that she was too critical to move.

Krystin and Kent came down because of Bev's hospitalization. Krystin introduced herself to the nurse, whose countenance paled. He thought she was Christina. (The word apparently had gotten around.) Between the two of them, they kept the medical staff alerted to Bev's needs.

As I mentioned, I was focused on finishing my projects at work. I knew Christina and Krystin would watch out for Bev. Krystin called me in tears and said I needed to get to the hospital ASAP. Bev was in severe pain because of the bi-pap machine, was praying to die, and was fading fast. The Global Missions staff came together for prayer, and then I took off for the hospital.

I had about a forty-five-minute drive. The Lord and I talked. Well, I talked, and He listened. I knew He was still our Healer and our lives were in His hands. I knew the day would come I would have to say goodbye to my wife. We had already been to that point numerous times, but the Lord always had come through and amazed the doctors. If this were her time, I would not try to hang on to her. Heaven would be so much better than the pain she was in most days and certainly the pain compounded by illness. I didn't like the idea, but I knew His will was always the best. And, through my tears, I praised Him for the forty-five years we had had together.

I parked and rushed to Bev's room. As I neared her room, I heard laughter. I was confused. When I walked in, she was sitting up and talking to Krystin, Phyllis Jones, and the others in the room. I was shocked! I had tried to prepare myself for her passing. Instead, the Lord had done it again! Krystin said that right after she called me, she could see a visible change take place in her mother—that was right after the prayer in Global Missions.

Eventually Bev was moved to Barnes-Jewish Hospital downtown and into the care of her regular doctors who had followed her medically for many years. She was finally released to a rehab center at the end of the year and spent the first two weeks of 2017 at the center, going through therapy and regaining her strength. She was doing better but was not bouncing back as quickly as she wanted. We took it easy for the rest of the year.

Chapter 20

Krystin's View

Being called by your sister-in-law to get to Mom's bedside immediately is something I should have been used to, but it never got easier. Kent and I rushed to Christian Northeast Hospital and found my mom on a bi-pap machine, struggling to breathe. Christina explained what was happening and that we needed to get her moved to Barnes where her doctors were. Trusting Christina and knowing she was millions percent correct, she and I began a campaign to move Mom. (Fun fact: doctors don't like being told to move a patient just because they don't have the experience to handle said patient.) Little deterred either of us. I spent many nights during that visit with Mom. She'd fight the breathing machines, tear off her mask, and then, unable to breathe, set off the alarms.

Soon doctors wanted to put her on a ventilator. All of us—Kent, Christina, Dad, and me—agreed Mom would never come off it. And she needed to get to BARNES! Each night as she struggled more and more, I started to sing

"Breathe of God." Of course, I could only remember two lines, but I sang those over and over and over.

I also wanted Mom to know I loved her. I thanked her for all the things she had taught me. I shared how I was able to survive my own horrible diseases because of her strength. Basically, I didn't want anything left unsaid.

One morning, Mom turned even more critical than she had been before. I looked at Christina who said, "Call Dad now!" I stepped outside the hospital room to call my dad and tell him to get up fast because it didn't look good at all. Then I called my husband and couldn't say a word. I just started crying hysterically.

As I was outside still crying on the phone with Kent, Phyllis Jones, a long-time mentor of mine, walked up. I hung up the phone and sobbed in her arms. We went in to pray and within minutes, Mom started to improve dramatically. Little did I know, the Global Missions staff had prayed before Dad left work. My husband also set prayer teams in South Bend to work. By the time, Daddy entered the room, I felt kinda silly as Mom was sitting up talking. I looked at him and said, "I promise she was really in bad shape!"

Christina moved mountains with the hospitals, and Mom was moved to Barnes. Once she was stable, I went back to South Bend. I left humming those two lines and praising God for miracles.

Chapter 21

Dorsey: 2018

In March 2018, Bev began feeling poorly. She was swabbed for flu—and that came back negative. She had an x-ray for pneumonia—and that too came back negative. Still, she wasn't feeling well.

A week later, Bev's home health nurse came for her weekly visit to draw blood and assess Bev's general health. Abby discovered discoloration in the IV catheter and called the doctor. The doctor told us to go to the ER.

On that Monday afternoon, Bev was admitted to Barnes-Jewish with bacteria in both her IV line and blood; she had sepsis. She also tested positive for pneumonia, Flu A, and Flu B. (She was much sicker than I thought!) The doctors pulled her central IV line and put her on strong IV antibiotics. After a few days, Intervention Radiology put a new IV line in. By Thursday, Bev had developed congestive heart failure. By Saturday, she was on the mend. The following Thursday they sent her to a nursing facility for rehab. However, Bev and the rehab center were not a good fit. On Saturday morning I checked her out and brought her home. I figured I could take better care of her.

A couple of weeks later at the follow-up visit with her primary care physician, the doctor explained that the intervention radiologist had to use a pediatric catheter because the *only* site left for a central line was a very small vein. The radiologist said it was *absolutely* the last site available. No more sites were available because of the past twenty-five years of scarring and damage to the blood vessels in the chest cavity. They were *all* blocked off. Bev had survived only because her heart had developed collateral veins.

The primary care doctor went on to say, "The new IV line will get infected; it's not a question of *if* but *when*. When that happens, the line will have to be pulled and you [Bev] will not have access to any supplemental fluids. Therefore, you will dehydrate, your kidneys will fail, and you will die."

That captured our attention. Doctors had told us years ago that the number of possible sites for an IV line were getting fewer. However, until this point, a new line was always possible.

Because of the pending medical catastrophe, the doctor advised us to see a vascular surgeon, a renal specialist, and a gastroenterologist so *together* they would have time to devise a plan to keep Bev alive after the IV line became infected.

The vascular surgeon explained he could improvise a way whereby she could have dialysis by using a vein and artery in the thigh. I guess this was supposed to be reassuring, but it wasn't. What good is dialysis if she is severely dehydrated? The kidney specialist was more relaxed. He said the situation might be years in the future and that Bev looked fifty-eight instead of sixty-eight. Translated, that means he didn't have any solutions to the pending disaster. The gastroenterologist, however, gave us hope.

Doctor Todorzcuk has been Bev's gastroenterologist for many years. When we told her what the primary said, she told us about a new drug designed to cause the villi in the intestine to elongate, thus increasing absorption. Immediately she asked her secretary to fill out the forms to see if Bev would qualify.

Within days the drug rep contacted Bev and set up an appointment to meet with us. She filled out more paperwork and said she was confident Bev would be approved for the Gattex. She also told us about a foundation that would possibly pay for all expenses related to the drug.

After Bev had been on the medication for over a week, definite signs indicated that the medication was working. Her ostomy output slowed and thickened. She felt warm and even sweated. Before she had always felt chilly, even during the hot St. Louis summers. It wasn't long until the infusion company reduced her nightly fluids by a third.

Chapter 22

For Bev: Gattex

Being told that I didn't have any more veins took away my hope of staying on my fluids. One time, due to insurance problems, I had been off my fluids and only lasted a few days before needing hospitalization. My greatest fear had been dying of thirst. The idea of not having IV fluids to keep me hydrated felt like a blow.

One doctor even said we needed to consider calling in hospice. I was blown away. I kept the news to just Dorsey and me for a few days. Eventually, I got the strength to tell the kids. I tried to keep it light and hopeful. Krystin saw right through that. "Mom, what aren't you tell me?" she asked.

Finally, I broke down in tears. I was scared to death. The word *hospice* was harder to take than hearing I had no more viable veins. Using my own words against me, Krystin asked what could I do about it right then? Worrying would make me worse and hadn't I taught the kids to trust?

After getting off the phone, I started to make a bucket list. If doctors were going to call in hospice, I had a few last things to do! Thankfully, only one doctor ended up feeling like hospice was needed. The others were more positive. I called Krystin back to tell her to relax. Inside, I was terrified.

When I told Dr. Todorzcuk what the radiologist had said about no more sites for another catheter, she mentioned a new drug that had recently been approved. She felt like I was a good candidate for it, and she set things in motion. It was designed to regrow parts of my intestines. The goal would be to increase the absorption rate so I wouldn't need my nightly fluids. I would be normal. This could be my miracle.

Despite it all, the company approved me for the drug! I was so happy, but the cost was overwhelming. Now I needed a miracle for the funding. Thankfully, God had it all worked out. The drug rep told us about a foundation that might pay all costs associated with the medicine. Dorsey and I filled out the application, and we were approved within a week or so. Dorsey and I rejoiced for another miracle!

Now it was time to tell the kids. When I called Krystin, she didn't answer so I left a message:

Krystin, this is Mom. I just wanted you to know the foundation that we contacted about paying for the Gattex has approved us. I am so excited right now that I can't even think about acting excited because I am too excited to get involved! I am just so grateful! Talk to you later. Bye, Bye

I started the medicine with hope and apprehension. I was their oldest patient. I had had Crohn's the longest.

And I had the least amount of intestines of those who would be taking it. In addition, I couldn't believe this would work. I tried to believe, but I was a bit scared.

Yet as time when on, I was seeing evidence the drug was working. I was putting out thicker waste. I had to use the restroom more. And, unbelievably, I started to sweat. While this may not be a miracle to some, it was huge to me. I used blankets and Cuddle Duds even in the worst of St. Louis's humid and hot summers.

After blood work, I was told I could reduce my fluids to every other night. I was in shock. I did, and I was fine.

Dorsey and I started to talk about traveling without taking my many bags of IV's and all the many things included. I dreamt of expanding our missions travels.

Finally, all my praise was worth it. Each morning, tears flowed down my face as I spent time with God. I praised Him for many hours and dreamed of teaching overseas. I started to get energy I thought I had lost. I had placed my life in His hands, and He provided a way none of us could have foreseen.

Although the meds were doing great things, I was extremely nauseous. I couldn't do things I wanted because I was fighting not to throw up. I refused to take extra meds unless I had to. I kept waiting for this side effect to pass.

Chapter 23

Dorsey: Victory

Naturally, the news that Bev's had no more sites available for another catheter was hard to take. I knew that we just had to trust God to either complete the healing or provide another viable vein. However, with the Gattex seemingly working and Bev's fluids being reduced, we thought that Gattex might be the miracle we needed.

Bev and I were planning on flying to Poland for ministry in Slovakia and Ukraine. The fluids being reduced by one-third was a welcome sign to us. When they further reduced her fluids to every other night, we got excited and began to think that perhaps we would not have to take any IV bags with us.

On Thursday, October 18, I picked missionaries Kirby and Mary Parker up at the airport. Bev joined us at McAllister's for lunch. After eating, the four of us went to the Sanctuary in Hazelwood, Missouri, to help set up for the Global Mission ConNEXTion, which is a meeting designed to promote short-term missions programs.

Dinning with Kirby and Mary Parker at Grbic in St. Louis

We were at the Sanctuary Thursday, Friday, and Saturday for services and for Saturday's "Lunch with Missionaries." Saturday evening we took the Parkers to Grbic, a Bosnian restaurant former missionary George Szabolsci had recommended.

On Sunday we were at both services at New Life St. Louis for Celebration of Nations Sunday. Monday evening we joined the Mike Tuttles, the Kirby Parkers, the Robert McFarlands, and the Gary Trumans for dinner to celebrate the Parkers and McFarlands's outbound orientations. Tuesday morning I took the Parkers back to the airport for their flight to Arizona. That evening Bev's nurse came to draw blood and assess her health. Life was continuing as usual.

The next morning, Bev woke me up about 3:30. She had been throwing up since about 2:30 and could not get up

Bev wore her Sri Lankan sari for Celebration of Nation Sunday at New Life St. Louis.

from the bathroom to go back to bed. She was in severe abdominal pain. Around 4:30, I helped her walk to the car and drove her to the ER at Missouri Baptist Hospital as her gastroenterologist practiced there.

On the way, I prayed that we would not have a long wait in the ER. I wheeled her in and no one else was in the waiting room. I answered a few questions for the intake nurse, who then excused me to move the car. By the time I returned, Bev was already in a room with four nurses getting the vital signs, drawing blood, hooking up IVs, and getting her gowned. In a couple of minutes, a doctor was on site. God answered my prayer.

The initial diagnosis was ischemic bowel. That meant Bev's six feet of remaining small intestine was either dead or dying due to lack of blood flowing to it. Her pain was intense. Finally, they gave her fentanyl, and she got some relief. Eventually, she was moved to a private room.

The gastroenterologist came and talked to me in the afternoon. The situation was grave. Normally the condition requires immediate surgery. However, the colorectal surgeon did not think Bev would survive the surgery because of her heart. And if surgery was performed, they would need to remove the remaining intestine. Dr. Todorzcuk suggested I notify the family and she asked about a living will and medical directives. Even though she did not directly say so, I knew she was trying to prepare me for the worst.

Bev's pain was unbearable. Fentanyl can't be given on the hospital floor, so they gave Bev morphine and dilaudid, both of which makes her extremely nauseated. However, Bev's white blood count and the lactic acid level were normal. This was a good sign that the intestine was not dead. I began to have hope that Bev would experience another miracle. But then her kidneys began to fail.

I stayed at the hospital Wednesday and Thursday nights. Krystin stayed with Bev Friday night; she was giving me a birthday present of a night of rest in my own bed.

During the night, Krystin heard Bev speaking in tongues. But even with the morphine and dilaudid, Bev continued to cry out because of the pain. Hospital policy requires that the patient must personally request pain medication. Bev was too sedated or comatose to do that. Consequently, we called for hospice on Saturday, and she was moved to the palliative care floor. The nurses there were so caring and helpful!

We recognized God was still the Healer. He could heal on the palliative care floor as well as on the regular medical floor. However, it seemed that He had better plans for Bev. By this time, she was unable to communicate. However, three different times she distinctly said she needed to get her hair washed. One of the last, if not the last, thing she said was, "I'm done." She knew her work on earth was finished.

As reality set in, each family member said his or her goodbye. As the word got out, friends and members of New Life St. Louis filled with hospital room.

One of the most touching scenes to me was the Sunday evening that three young ladies from New Life came by to pay their respects. Each one told Bev how she had helped her through a very trying time in her life. Bev had embraced each one, imparted words of divine wisdom, and given a warm hug that changed their lives. That was a side of Bev that many did not know, and even I did not know these specific details.

Bev did not want to die at home or in the hospital. About noon on Tuesday, October 30, the ambulance arrived to transport Bev to Evelyn's House, a hospice center. During her frequent visits to Dr. Nordlicht's office, Bev had watched the construction of the facility as it was near his office. As she was being transferred from the ambulance's gurney to the bed in her room, she entered the land of no tears and no pain. It was 12:37 PM.

In keeping with Bev's expressed desires, she was cremated. A memorial service was held in her honor at 7:00 PM, Friday, November 9, 2018, at New Life St. Louis, Bridgeton, Missouri. The New Life praise team encapsulated the service by singing Richard Smallwood's "Total Praise":

Lord, I will lift my eyes to the hills
Knowing my help is coming from You
Your peace You give me in time of the storm

You are the source of my strength
You are the strength of my life
I lift my hands in total praise to You

You are the source of my strength
You are the strength of my life
I lift my hands in total praise to You

Amen, Amen, Amen, Amen
Amen, Amen, Amen, Amen

Her obituary states:

Beverly (Bev) Jeannene Sponsler Burk was born on July 24, 1950, to George and Verna Barton Sponsler in Visalia, California. She graduated from Conquerors Bible College in 1971 and married

Dorsey Burk June 26, 1971. On October 14, 1972, they welcomed Krystin Michelle to the family and rejoiced at the birth of Devon Paul on May 2, 1976. Krystin and Kent Carlson made Bev a doting grandmother with the birth of Abigayle Leann (Mrs. Jordan Sneff) followed by Rebekka Michelle (Mrs. David Aaron DelaRosa). Devon and Christina added Alexis Alice, Crysellyn René, Javan Paul, and Samara Christine. Great granddaughter Kaidyn Jhené Burk quickly stole Bev's heart in 2015.

On October 13, 1973, Bev, Dorsey, and Krystin landed in Kingston, Jamaica, to begin a lifelong commitment to missions. She and Dorsey taught in Caribbean Bible Institute, in Kingston, and fell in love with the island and its people. In October 1976, Bev was diagnosed with Crohn's disease, an incurable intestinal disease. In October 1977, Dorsey and Bev were appointed as United Pentecostal Church missionaries to West Germany. However, Bev's illness forced them home in March 1981.

When Dorsey became an executive assistant in Global Missions in January 1982, the family moved back to St. Louis. At the urging of the principal of Krystin and Devon's elementary school, Bev enrolled in Missouri Baptist College and received her BSE in Education in 1989. She was the fifth generation of educators and excelled in the classroom. Her disease forced her from her own classroom in 1993, but she substituted when her health permitted.

As Bev's health became more "stable," she joined the staff of Global Missions, first as a volunteer and later became the division's receptionist. Many of the visiting missionaries and other guests considered her to be the welcoming "face" of Global Missions, for hers was the first smile that greeted them as they stepped out of the third-floor elevator. Bev retired from Global Missions in September 2016.

Bev's passion was missions. Most of her annual vacations were spent ministering overseas in such places as Poland, Serbia, Germany, Malta, and Sri Lanka. She and Dorsey were planning to leave to teach and preach in Slovakia and Ukraine on November 13. However, intense intestinal pain and a trip to the Emergency Room at Missouri Baptist Hospital in the early hours of October 24 changed their plans. God had a better itinerary for Bev. She boarded her flight to Heaven at 12:37 on the afternoon of October 30.

Bev Burk: Daughter of the Most High God, wife, mother, grandmother, great grandmother, missionary, mentor, teacher, role model, voice of wisdom, listening ear, and tear-absorbing shoulder. For over forty years Bev stated she had a disease but was not sick. Through it all, her priority in life was praising her Savior. And now she is healed! Her new body has no scars, no pain, and no IVs. She's in the presence of the King.

Chapter 24

Krystin's View

My dad called on Wednesday to tell me he once again had to take Mom to the hospital. The doctor was advising Kent, who had Mom's medical power of attorney, and the family to arrive quickly. Bags were thrown together. I looked at Kent and said, although I am not sure why, "I think we need to bring funeral clothes."

Kent made a phone call to our pastor, James McKinnies, who placed my parents and my family on the prayer phone list. In addition, Kent called his parents who decided they would drive us down to St. Louis. This was such a blessing as my mother-in-law, Floydene Jo Carlson, kept all of our laundry done and cooked all the meals for us.

We spent hours at the hospital, and my dad was exhausted. I sent him home Friday night as it seemed Mom was fairly stable, and he needed to sleep in his own bed.

My sister-in-law Christina came very late after her nursing shift to spend time with Mom. We talked to Mom and shared stories. Christina said about a month ago Mom was asking her and the kids questions she'd never asked before. *How is your walk with God? Do you think you're ok with God?* Mom had never been so blunt or intrusive.

Mom alternated between moaning in pain and speaking in tongues. Christina and I just prayed and praised with her. Christina leaned in and said, "Mom, I kept you from going to Heaven and getting your full miracle five years ago. I am stronger now. I'm okay. I promise. You can go home now."

I sat in awe as tears rolled down my face and I bawled. Christina kissed Mom and left for her early nursing shift.

Thinking Christina had the right idea, I also talked to Mom. We'd talked about so many things I didn't have much left but one critical promise: "Mom, I promise that I will teach the next generation and my own grandchildren to praise when there appears to be nothing to praise for. Your hard-learned lessons will continue. I promise."

That night was one of the worst of my life. Mom was screaming in pain and I couldn't help her. Prayer helped for a short time but only a short time. She'd yell, "I want to go home." The entire night was filled with incoherent moaning. I played praise music on my phone just to remind me to praise. It was obvious she was speaking in tongues at times, but she was also out of her mind more and more as the night went on. Since Mom couldn't talk and ask for pain meds, she couldn't have them.

Dad came in early that morning. Doctors came in and said Mom was dying. There was no other way to put it. It was clearer and clearer something had to be done for her comfort.

Kent, Christina, Dad, and I spent awhile talking and reviewing Mom's advance medical directive.

Then we called in the grandkids. Each of the six talked to her. During one of the kids' conversations, they must have said something about going to Jesus or seeing her in Heaven, because all the sudden in a very loud, strong voice, Mom said, "NOT UNITL MY HAIR IS WASHED." There was complete silence and then pure laughter. It was such a Bev Burk moment for the family.

Despite moving Mom to the hospice floor at the hospital, she hung on to life. Kent said Mom probably didn't know how to die since she had been fighting most of her adult life to live.

With her hair washed, Mom went to see God on Tuesday, October 30, 2018.

Chapter 26

Krystin: A Lesson and a Promise

My parents were my rock. I watched my parents praise, but please understand that praise was not a first instinct. They were human. I saw the stress of bills, pain, long hospital stays, and long weeks of having to be a single father. Despite the trauma of being a part of a family with a chronically ill mother, I have great memories.

My favorite of my father is waking up in the middle of the night. Once again, Mom was in the hospital. I don't remember my age, but I must have been around twelve. I wasn't sure what woke me up, but I heard what sounded like crying. I got up thinking maybe my brother needed me. Instead, I found my dad sitting in a very old recliner, praying and literally sobbing to God. To this day, I remember just a few of his words: "I am trying to praise, God. I am trying to praise."

I should have gone back to bed. I should have given my daddy the privacy he needed, but I didn't. I sat down, leaned against the hallway wall, and learned the greatest prayer lesson of my life. Praise isn't easy. It's an exhausting wrestling match. But once you can praise, you can rest in knowing God will fight the rest of the battle for you.

Mom had one last lesson for me.

As I've said before, my parents have been my rock. Along with my husband, they supported me through the craziness of my own disease. So, it wasn't a surprise to Mom and Dad when I called them early in the summer of 2018 to get some advice.

The pastor of our church had died quite suddenly, despite our twenty-four-hour fasting and praying and seemingly positive promises. I praised God for seeing the future and knowing what was best for our church. I did all the "right things" that I had been taught my whole life, yet my bitterness seemed to grow. I can't say I was angry at God, but I was certainly angry at the lack of a miracle. I called my mom and dad, who were traveling in the South. On the speakerphone, I shared my thoughts, which were disjointed and filled with tears, but as usual my parents understood. My mom said, "Well, Krys, I don't have an answer right now but let Dad and me pray, and I'll call you back."

About five or ten minutes later, my phone rang. Mom said, "Krys, this is what I think God wants you to do. You need to fall back in love with God."

"Wait," I interrupted, "I still love God." (I was as defensive as it sounds.) Mom said, "I didn't say you didn't love God. I said you need to fall back IN LOVE with God.

Here's what you're going to do. For one week, you are going to not ask for one thing. You can't ask your friends to pray for you. You can't allude to needing prayer. Nothing. During this week, you are going to spend an hour each day researching the character of God, journal about it, and then praise for each one." I really wasn't sure this was going to help, but I promised and thought it would be an easy assignment.

Of course, that week things fell apart. One son-in-law had an accident at work and needed emergency surgery. My other son-in-law was applying to join the Air Force. My girls needed a praying momma! So many other things fell apart, but I kept my promise.

I did the normal characters of God at first: Good, faithful, and so forth. Then I got stuck and started to "research." It was a very private time, one I didn't even share with my husband or kids. On the third day, I fell on my knees and fell in love with God again. Was I still hurting? Oh yes! Was I broken as I watched my friend struggle with the loss of her husband? Again, oh yes! But I remembered all over again that God is love.

It wasn't long after that that Mom and Dad came up. Mom must have known she was going Home, as she went through a list of all the family members and why they'd be "okay" when she went Home. She went fishing again with my husband, a "bucket list" item for her. We had conversation after conversation about her being tired of fighting and ready to go Home.

In typical mom style, she kept adding she wasn't going until after her cruise to Alaska. We laughed a lot and made memories as usual. She lectured as my own neurological diseases showed up. She'd often ask, "What can you do about it, Krys? Worrying is only going to make you worse." This is a phrase my own daughters hear now. But she was right.

I cried almost every night, knowing this time was different than normal. As it turns out, that visit was different.

On October 30, 2018, my life changed. I no longer have daily phone calls or texts with my mom. What I do have is a promise to impart her legacy of praise on to the next generation. As long as there is praise being raised when it's very dark, she lives on. As long as there is praise as the miracle gets closer and closer, she lives on. As long as there is praise when the miracle is in sight and present, she lives on. When my children—all four of them—praise in the hard times, my mom and their grandmother lives on.

Praise isn't just a word; it's a lifestyle.

Chapter 26

Dorsey: An Afterword

(Author's Note: This is an updated version of the Afterword that appeared in the original book copyrighted in 2000.)

The miracle that Bev and I anticipated did not occur as we had hoped. However, her miracle is even greater, for she has joined the heavenly host in continually praising God. It is simply the outgrowth of a very important lesson she learned as a young missionary in Wiesbaden, Germany. Because of praise, her life was changed.

Bev's life continues to amaze me. Her drive to live and to do astounds me. She was a substitute elementary teacher for a suburban St. Louis public school district. She coordinated volunteers for the World Network of Prayer and was active in the prayer ministry at New Life St. Louis, Bridgeton, Missouri. She was a devoted wife, mother, grandmother, and great-grandmother. She filled each role with creativity, sincerity, and class. I was privileged to be her husband.

I often wonder how our lives would have been if I were the one afflicted with Crohn's instead of her. Would I have given up the fight long ago? Would I have caved in to the pain and become so self-centered that all I cared about was how I feel? Would I have been as caring and giving as she was? I hope I am never tested to find out.

Years ago, Mickey Mangun penned the following song, which is used by permission:

> When I made my start for heaven
> I could only find one way,
> A road that led me through
> The mountains and valleys,
> A road not many folks could take.
> Since I started traveling on my journey
> I've covered many, many miles behind me,
> Miles of sun and rain,
> Miles of smiles and pain.
> This road's been rough
> But I again would choose the same.
>
> Long and winding road keep on leading me.
> Up ahead I see a sign that tells me
> You're headed straight for your victory.
> I know I must be traveling right
> For I remember passing Calvary.
> Although it's dusty and it's old,
> For years it's borne the traveler's load;
> Someday this road will turn to gold.
>
> There are sometimes when the rocks hurt my feet;
> My body burns from the sweat and heat

> My strength completely drains
> Until my face marks the pain.
> My back gets bent from the strain.
> Now I could turn around,
> For the road is still back there.
> But every mountain that I've climbed
> I would again have to bear,
> So, I really can't turn back.
> Some may be using my tracks.
> I see one more bend,
> And that just might be the old road's end.

What a wonderful song to describe our odyssey! *Miles of sun and rain. Miles of smiles and pain.* Our long and winding road was not one that I would have willingly chosen for us—or anyone else. However, God, in His love and mercy, chose it for us. An easier road may have allowed us to grow spiritually lax and indifferent. A harsher path may have been too steep and discouraging. So, God in His infinite wisdom and boundless goodness chose a road that led us *through the mountains and valleys, a road not many folks could take.* He knew the trail that was perfectly suited to cause us to draw close to Him.

And now, *up ahead I see a sign that tells me we're headed straight for victory*. Yes, the road's been ever so long and dusty. The load's been almost unbearable. But Jesus has walked beside us. When our strength was completely drained and our faces were marked with pain, He was there to empower us and to lift the load. And so, *this road's been rough, but I again would choose the same.*

Choose the same?! Yes. I have no desire to repeat the course. However, when I consider the beauty along the way and how the path has transformed us, I must freely admit that His choice was best. The path He chose was based on His love for us and His desire that we should be conformed to His nature. And even though I may have been tempted to seek an easier way, I know that He selected the best route *for us*. The best part of the journey has been realizing that He is always there. He has proven Himself faithful time and time again. At times I could only see His shadow. In the darkness of some nights, I could only hear Him faintly calling my name. But at other times, His glory illuminated the rocky trail and led to scenic vistas.

Bev's journey has ended in victory. She has a new body free of pain, scars, and ostomy bags. She rejoices around the Throne, praising God eternally.

However, my odyssey continues. Oh, how I miss my traveling partner! The path seems rockier without her. And so, I cling more desperately to my Guide. Thankfully, up ahead *I see one more bend, and that just might be this old road's end. . . . Someday this road will turn to gold.*

So, until then, I will "praise Him with the joy that comes from knowing [we] have held back nothing and He is Lord.

That's the promise I made to Bev. And God, that's what I promise You.

Made in the USA
Lexington, KY
22 March 2019